SECOND EDITION **5**
Workbook

Herbert Puchta · Peter Lewis-Jones · Günter Gerngross · Helen Kidd

CAMBRIDGE
UNIVERSITY PRESS

Contents

The Science lesson

1 Look and write the words.

① goggles

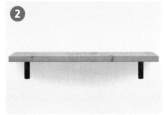

②

③

④

⑤

⑥

⑦

⑧

2 Read and complete the text.

Wednesday, 5ᵗʰ September

Alex, Phoebe and Patrick were in the **(1)** Science_____ lab_____.

I was near the window. All three were wearing **(2)** g_____ on

their hands. Phoebe and Alex were also wearing **(3)** g_____, but

Patrick wasn't. His **(4)** g_____ were on a **(5)** s_____. Patrick

was holding the **(6)** t_____ t_____ in his left hand. With his

right hand, he put two **(7)** s_____ of blue **(8)** p_____ in the

(9) t_____ t_____. Then there was an **(10)** e_____.

Lots of **(11)** b_____ came out of the **(12)** t_____ t_____. Then Mr Davis went

to talk to them.

He was angry. He told Patrick to put on his **(13)** g_____. When Mr Davis left, he said to

me, 'John, get back to your place.' So I left. I didn't see what happened in the **(14)** S_____

l_____ afterwards. That's all I can say.

John

1 Complete with the correct form of each verb.

Language focus

Listen friends, to what I say.

1 Yesterday _____ (be) a perfect day.

2 I _____ (get out) of bed at half past three.

3 I _____ (see) a chicken under the tree.

2 Write the verbs in the correct column. Write the base form of the verbs.

~~looked~~ ~~came~~ found started played heard laughed ran walked told waited arrived said loved took watched had went

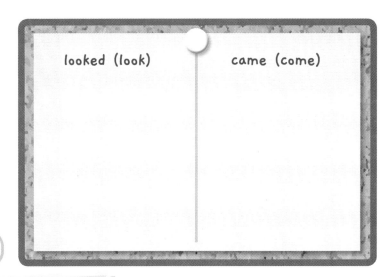

looked (look)   came (come)

3 Look at the pictures. Write the story.

~~had~~ laughed arrived ran rode had

Last night, Susan had a dream.

_____

_____

1   **Listen to the song again and complete with the words in the box.**

come back   future   last   cross   ~~want~~   late   followed   mate   wait

Phoebe was the first one,
She didn't **(1)** ___want___ to **(2)** _____.
Now she's lost in time because
She stepped into that gate.

Alex **(3)** _____ Phoebe
Because he's her best **(4)** _____.
Now he's lost in time because
He stepped into that gate.

Patrick was the **(5)** _____ one,
But then, he's always **(6)** _____.
Now he's lost in time because
He stepped into that gate.

The Time Travellers,
They're lost in time,
They'll never **(7)** _____
If they **(8)** _____ that line.

The Time Travellers,
Travelling so fast,
The past is the present,
And the **(9)** _____ is the past.

2 **Listen and say the words.**

zoo   you

3 **Match the rhyming words.**

1 zoo	c		**a**	great
2 say	___		**b**	come
3 mum	___		**c**	~~you~~
4 see	___		**d**	grey
5 wait	___		**e**	one
6 fly	___		**f**	friend
7 too	___		**g**	fruit
8 sun	___		**h**	I
9 end	___		**i**	through
10 boot	___		**j**	me

Phonics tip
Some words are easy to say because the spelling helps you. Look for rhymes to help you say more difficult words.

4 **Listen, check and say the words.**

1 Read and complete.   Did   How   have   was

1 _____ _____ your day, Leo?

2 _____ you _____ fun?

No, I didn't, Mum. I had none.

2 Match the questions with the answers.

1 What did you do at school today?   [e]

2 Did you like the film?   [ ]

3 What was it about?   [ ]

4 That's interesting. When did they live?   [ ]

5 Where did they live?   [ ]

6 How long was the film?   [ ]

7 Why didn't you see the whole film?   [ ]

a   Yes, it was great.

b   About 700 years ago.

c   Because it was longer than the lesson.

d   I don't know. We didn't see the whole film.

e   ~~We watched a film in Geography.~~

f   The Aztecs.

g   In Mexico.

3 Make questions.

1 happen / did / When / accident / the / ?
   When did the accident happen?

2 did / you / put / goggles / Where / your / ?
   _____
   _____

3 was / test tube / What / the / in / ?
   _____
   _____

4 wear / in / Science lab / Did / gloves / you / the / ?
   _____
   _____

5 you / Why / teacher / angry / Science / was / the / with / ?
   _____
   _____

4 Read and write the questions.

1 **What did you do on Saturday?**
   On Saturday? Holly and I did an experiment.

2 _____
   At Holly's place. In the cellar.

3 _____
   We tried to make gold.

4 _____
   No, it wasn't dangerous. There were a few
   bubbles, but no explosion.

5 _____
   Then we asked Holly's father to help us.

6 _____
   He showed us how to make special ink for
   secret messages.

1 🛡 **Remember the story. Read and order.**

☐ A strange yellow gate appears.

☐ Phoebe can't read the instructions.

☐ There is a red flash.

☐ The children make a brick get bigger.

☐ Mr Davis talks to the children.

☐ Alex puts different coloured powders into a test tube.

1 Phoebe adds the yellow powder to the blue liquid.

☐ Patrick starts doing an experiment.

2 🛡 **Complete the sentences with the correct names.**

1 _Phoebe_ turns the red brick purple.

2 _____ doesn't think the experiment is very exciting.

3 _____ follows Patrick's instructions.

4 _____ tells them to read the instructions carefully.

5 _____ knocks over a bottle of water.

6 _____ and _____ don't laugh at the explosion.

3 **Complete the instructions and the answers to the questions.**

Experiment 1

• Add one spoon of **(1)** _____yellow_____ powder to the blue liquid.

• Add a few drops of the liquid (which should now be **(2)** _____) to the red brick.

What happens to the brick?

(3) _____
_____

Experiment 2

• Take a test tube and put in **(4)** _____ spoons of white powder and one spoon of **(5)** _____ powder.

• Add some **(6)** _____ liquid into the test tube.

• Now pour some of the liquid (which should now be **(7)** _____) onto the brick.

What happens to the brick?

(8) _____
_____

4 Complete the Chemistry sums. Write and draw, then colour.

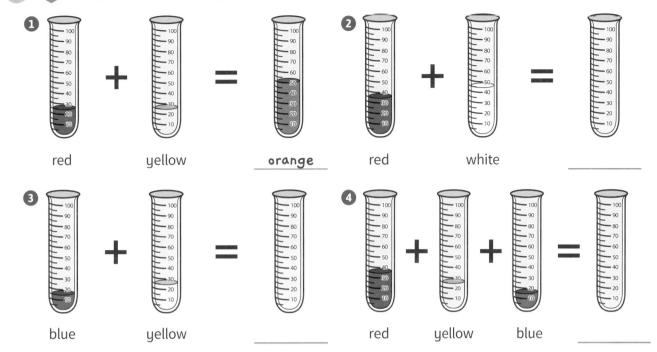

1 red + yellow = __orange__

2 red + white = _____

3 blue + yellow = _____

4 red + yellow + blue = _____

5 What are the students doing wrong? Look, read and write the sentences. Use the words from the box.

apron   goggles   gloves   ~~instructions~~

1 __She isn't following the instructions.__

2 _____

3 _____

4 _____

6 Write what the teacher says to the children in Activity 5.

1 Read the instructions.

2 _____

3 _____

4 _____

1 Look and complete.

1

v o l c a n o

2

f __ u __ t __ i __

3

c __ l __ m __

4

horse and c __ r __

5

t __ e __ t __ e

6

s __ a __ u __

7

s __ r __ a __ t

8

v __ s __

9

s __ o __ e

10

t __ m __ l __

2 Do the crossword.

```
                                    1
                            2s  t  a  3t  u  e
              4        5                              6
        7                                      8
      9
```

Across

2 ~~A person or animal made of stone.~~

7 A mountain with a large hole at the top.

8 You put flowers and water in it.

9 Water is pushed up into the air from it.

Down

1 They work for other people.

2 You get it when you make a fire.

3 People go there to see a play.

4 A tall stone post.

5 Horses pull it.

6 The house of a god or gods.

3 Complete with the words from the box and the past tense of the verbs in brackets.

> cart   columns   fountain   ~~servant~~
> smoke   statue   theatre   volcano

1 The **servant bought** (buy) lots of food.

2 Phoebe _____ (think) that the _____ was Vesuvius.

3 Patrick and Alex _____ (admire) the _____ of a man.

4 Our friends _____ (go) to the _____ last night to see a play.

5 Two horses _____ (pull) a _____.

6 The temple _____ (be) a big building with lots of stone _____.

7 Phoebe _____ (drink) the water from the _____.

8 The boys were scared because they _____ (see) thick black _____.

1 **Read and complete.** [were   reading   playing   was]

When the earthquake shook the tree,
Leo **(1)** _____ _____ quietly.
When the earthquake shook the tree,
The monkeys **(2)** _____ _____ hide and seek.

2 **Write what the family was doing when there was an earthquake.**

[read   ~~cook~~   play   do   listen   watch]

1 Dad and Mum **were cooking** _____ .
2 Emily _____ .
3 Lily _____ .
4 The grandparents _____ .
5 Tom _____ .
6 Oliver _____ .

3 **What were you doing at the weekend? Write sentences about you.**

1 On Saturday morning at 10 o'clock, I
_____ .

2 At lunchtime, _____
_____ .

3 At 3 o'clock, _____
_____ .

4 At 6 o'clock, _____
_____ .

5 On Sunday morning at 11.30, _____
_____ .

6 At 2 o'clock, _____
_____ .

7 At 5 o'clock, _____
_____ .

4 **Look at Activity 1. Write two more lines for the poem.**

When the earthquake shook the tree,
_____

When the earthquake shook the tree,
_____

1 Remember the song. Look and complete the sentences.

1 He was <u>working in the garden when</u>
  <u>the ground began to shake</u>.

2 A statue _____.

3 He _____.

4 He was _____.

5 She was _____.

6 She looked _____.

7 She could see _____.

8 The volcano _____.

2 🎧 004 Listen and say the words.

cap   cape   cut   cute

Phonics tip

An *e* at the end of a word often makes the vowel sound long.

3 Complete the sentences.

lake   nine   smoke   tube
~~shakes~~   inside   safe   time

1 When there's an earthquake, the ground
  <u>shakes</u>.

2 What _____ is it?
  It's _____ o'clock.

3 Can you see the _____ from that fire?

4 Let's take our boat out on the _____.

5 It's starting to rain. Let's go _____.

6 Don't touch that wire. It isn't _____.

7 Put some green powder in the test _____.

4 🎧 005 Listen, check and say the sentences.

Word watch

Some words don't follow the pattern: *have, come.*

1 Order the words to make sentences.

Language focus

1 Leo / While / moon / looking / the / was / at / ,

_____

2 spoon / was / The / his / explorer / stealing / favourite / .

_____

3 Leo / lake / was / While / the / in / swimming / ,

_____

4 eating / cake / The / his / explorer / was / chocolate / .

_____

2 Read and match.

1 While Jessica was working in the garden, [c]

2 While Harry was watching TV, [ ]

3 While Sophie and Jack were fighting, [ ]

4 While Dad was [ ]

5 While our teacher was showing a [ ]

a their dog was hiding behind the curtains.

b sleeping, his little boy was painting the walls.

c ~~her dog was digging a big hole.~~

d film, Mark was sleeping.

e his dog was eating his birthday cake.

3 Look and write sentences about John and Ava.

1 While John was riding his bike, Ava was riding her skateboard.

2 _____

3 _____

4 _____

5 _____

6 _____

1 Remember the story. Put the pictures in order.

2 Read and use the words from the box to complete the text. There are four extra words.

| vase | erupts | gate | Pompeii | people | volcano |
| ~~hill~~ | statue | smoke | fountain | danger | column |

The children are in a strange city. Phoebe starts to run and she tells the boys to follow her. They run up a **(1)** _____hill_____. The boys don't understand. When they get to the top, Phoebe explains everything to the boys.

She tells them the city is called **(2)** _____. She shows them a **(3)** _____ called Vesuvius and says that it is going to erupt. There is a loud noise and lots of dark grey **(4)** _____ starts coming from the volcano. Then they see lots of animals running away from the volcano. Phoebe explains that animals often run away when there is **(5)** _____.
The children decide to go back to the city to tell the **(6)** _____ about the danger, but nobody understands them. The volcano **(7)** _____ and the children are very scared. Alex notices the yellow glowing **(8)** _____.
The children decide that it is their only escape. They jump through it and disappear.

3 Correct the sentences.

1 While Phoebe was running down the stairs, she told the ~~people in the market~~ **boys** to follow her.
2 While Alex and Patrick were following Phoebe, they ran past carts and horses.
3 When the children reached the top of the hill, they built a fire.
4 While Phoebe was telling the boys about Pompeii, they heard people shout.
5 When the children looked at the volcano, they saw a lot of animals.
6 While the children were trying to talk to the people, a statue fell down.
7 When the volcano exploded, the people were very angry.
8 While the children were thinking about what to do, Alex saw lots of birds in the sky.

4 Where will the children go next? Put these times in order of age. Start with the oldest.

1

5 Read. Which of the pictures is it about?

Picture: ☐

In my story, the children go to Egypt. They get lost in a pyramid and they have a really exciting adventure. The gate saves them at the end of the story.

6 Where would you like to send the children? Write three sentences.

In my story, _____

_____

_____

_____

_____

_____

7   What message can we learn from the story in the Student's Book? <u>Underline</u> the best summary.

a If there is danger, you should always run away quickly.

b If there is danger, you should tell other people quickly, if there is time.

c If there is danger, you should never help other people.

1 What natural disasters are the people talking about? Write the words.

1 It started at two o'clock in the morning. The whole house was shaking!

__an earthquake__

2 It snowed heavily for three days before the catastrophe happened.

_____

3 There was water everywhere. They had to rescue some people by helicopter.

_____

4 When the wind came up, the flames spread quickly. There are no trees left.

_____

5 The wind was very strong. It destroyed houses and cars, and several people were injured.

_____

2 Read the text on page 16 of the Student's Book again. Then complete the chart below.

CAUSED BY WEATHER:
hurricanes _____
_____ _____

NOT CAUSED BY WEATHER:
_____ _____

NATURAL DISASTERS

CAUSED BY PEOPLE TOO:
_____

THE MOST EXPENSIVE:
_____

3 Use the Internet to find out about one of the natural disasters below. Circle your choice and make notes.

	When / Where?	Danger
thunderstorms	often during hot summers, in many countries	lightning – wild fires can destroy houses
floods		
avalanches		
hurricanes		

4 Write three sentences about the disaster you chose in Activity 3.

_____

_____

_____

1 🎧 006 **Listen and draw lines. There is one example.**

Mr Roberts　　　　　　　Mr Richards　　　　　　　Harry

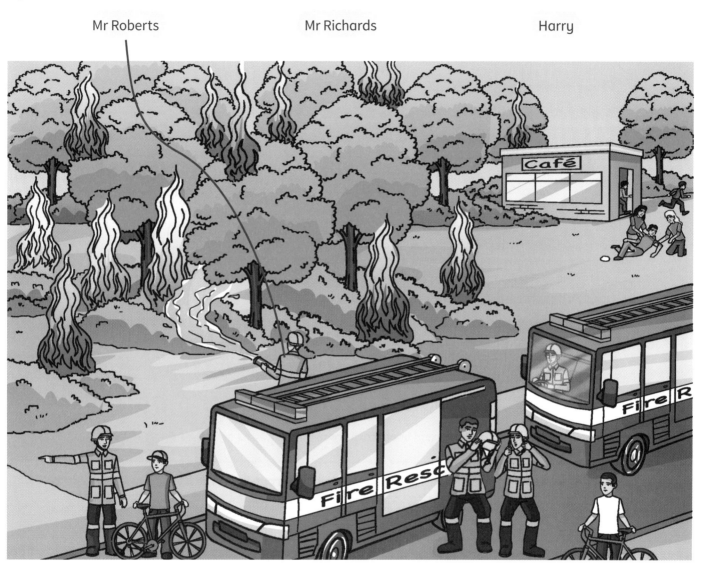

William　　　　　　　David　　　　　　　Helen

2 **Look and read. Write *yes* or *no*.**

1 All the trees are on fire.　　　　　　　　　　<u>　no　</u>

2 The fire isn't in the park.　　　　　　　　　<u>　　　　</u>

3 There are two fire engines in the street.　　<u>　　　　</u>

4 All the firemen are wearing helmets.　　　　<u>　　　　</u>

5 One fireman is talking to a boy on a skateboard.　<u>　　　　</u>

6 There are two boys with bikes.　　　　　　<u>　　　　</u>

7 A boy has a hurt knee.　　　　　　　　　　<u>　　　　</u>

8 Some people are running from a café in the park.　<u>　　　　</u>

9 One fireman is in a fire engine.　　　　　　<u>　　　　</u>

1 Look. Complete the sentences.

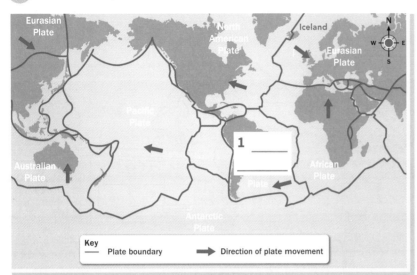

Key
— Plate boundary ➡ Direction of plate movement

| continental   earthquakes   erupt |
| ~~oceanic~~   South American |

2 The Pacific Plate is an ___oceanic___ plate.

3 The Eurasian Plate is mostly a _____ plate.

4 Lots of _____ happen in the 'Ring of Fire' around the Pacific Ocean.

5 Where two plates meet, volcanoes can _____.

2 Read, then write where the volcanoes are found.

FUN AND FIERY FACTS!

- The word 'volcano' comes from 'Vulcan', the Roman god of fire.

- When a volcano erupts, hot gas, ash and liquid rock come out of it, as well as pieces of solid rock.

- Hot liquid rock inside the Earth is called magma. When it comes out, it is called lava.

- Most volcanoes happen near plate boundaries, but some happen at 'hot spots' where there is very hot rock close to the Earth's surface – like Mt Kilauea, in Hawaii.

- Volcanoes can erupt on land, under the sea or under ice. There are more than 100 volcanoes in Iceland! Many of them erupt through the ice, like Eyjafjallajökull, which last erupted in 2010.

- Volcanoes can cause a lot of damage. Rocks can injure people and damage buildings. Lava can destroy buildings and trees. Volcanoes can melt ice, and the water can mix with rock and ash to make mudslides. The ash can travel a long way into the sky – sometimes more than 30 km!

- There are some big volcanoes on Earth, but there's a bigger one on Mars. It's called Olympus Mons, and it's 600 km wide and 21 km high. And Io, one of Jupiter's moons, is covered in volcanoes that are erupting all the time!

Olympus Mons is on
_____.

Mt Kilauea is in
_____.

Eyjafjallajökull is in
_____.

3 **Read and answer.**

Why do you think there are more than 100 volcanoes in Iceland? (Look at the map in Activity 1 for ideas!)

4 Read the article in Activity 2 again. Tick ✔ the true sentences.

1 Most volcanoes happen at plate boundaries. ☐

2 Mt Kilauea erupts because it is a 'hot spot'. ☐

3 Volcanoes only happen on continental plates. ☐

4 Eyjafjallajökull hasn't erupted in this century. ☐

5 We don't know if volcanoes happen on other planets. ☐

5 Write the phrases in the correct place.

under ice   injure people   solid rocks   ~~liquid rock (lava)~~   destroy buildings

under the sea   hot gas   make mudslides   hot ash   on land

Things that come out of volcanoes	Where volcanoes can erupt	Damage volcanoes do
liquid rock (lava)		

6 Project Complete the chart with information about the South American Plate. Then draw it on the map.

CITIES	_____ _____
VOLCANOES	_____ _____
EARTHQUAKES	_____ _____

Andes Mountains

South American Plate

7 Read and answer.

Look at the map in Activity 6. Why do you think the Andes Mountains are where they are?

Key
● city
▲ volcano
〜 earthquake

1 Draw lines and complete the sentences with the words from the box.

walked   I was   TV   ~~football~~   cleaning   volcano   its food

1 While he was playing	watching _____,	broke his leg.
2 While they were	up, Mum was	was eating _____.
3 While the _____	was sleeping, the cat	the phone rang.
4 While Dad was washing	_football_ , he	_____ into a window.
5 While the dog	was erupting, the villagers	_____ the kitchen.
6 While _____ walking	down the street, I	were sleeping.

2 Find the words and use them to complete the sentences.

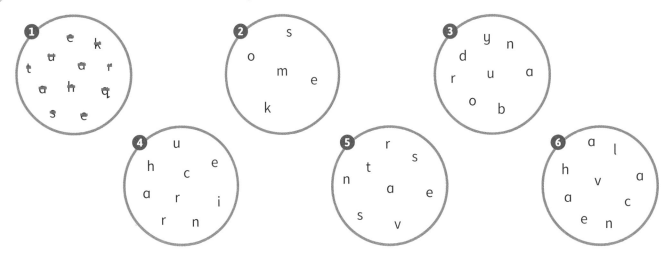

1 Around 90% of _____earthquakes_____ happen in the Ring of Fire.

2 Look! There's lots of _____ coming out of the volcano!

3 Most volcanoes happen near a plate _____.

4 The _____ blew the roofs off many houses and turned cars upside down.

5 The rich Romans had lots of _____ who worked for them.

6 We couldn't go skiing because there was a danger of an _____ in the mountains.

3 Complete the sentences with your own ideas.

1 While Mia was sleeping, _____.

2 While the friends were playing football, _____.

3 While our teacher was _____.

4 While I was _____.

What do I know?

1 **Read and tick ✓. Then write examples.**

1 I can use the past continuous to describe an action in the past. ☐

_____

2 I can use the past continuous with _while_ to describe two simultaneous actions. ☐

_____

3 I can write the names of five things in Pompeii. ☐

_____ _____ _____

_____ _____

2 🛡 **Write sentences to answer the Big Question.**

BIG QUESTION **What are natural disasters?**

_____

_____

_____

My story

3 🛡 **Look at the pictures. Imagine the man in the pictures is your neighbour, Mr Wilson. Write the story.**

Think about: what Mr Wilson was doing.

what the dog was doing.

what happened.

what you did.

_____

_____

_____

_____

_____

_____

_____

_____

_____

1 Find eight countries in the word search. Write them on the map. Look → and ↓.

1 _ _ _ n _ z _ _ _ _ _ _

2 _ _ _ y _ _ n _ _

3 _ _ u _ _ _ n _ _ _ e

4 _ _ _ l _ m b _ _ _

5 E c u a d o r

6 _ _ _ _ _ z _ _ _

7 _ _ e _ _ _ _

8 _ _ o _ _ _ _ i _

e	c	u	a	d	o	r	v	c	s
b	r	a	z	i	l	g	e	o	p
b	r	a	n	c	h	b	n	l	s
s	p	o	b	h	v	e	e	o	u
b	o	l	i	v	i	a	z	m	r
p	e	r	u	t	a	k	u	b	i
~~p~~	~~o~~	~~o~~	~~l~~	v	x	s	e	i	n
g	u	y	a	n	a	h	l	a	a
a	n	a	c	o	n	d	a	i	m
c	r	e	e	p	e	r	s	r	e

2 Find four more rainforest words in the word search in Activity 1. Write the words.

1 It's a place with water. _____pool_____

2 Part of a tree you can climb on.

_____

3 They hang from trees and animals can swing on them. _____

4 Birds eat with them. _____

5 It's a kind of snake. _____

3 Write the words in the correct column.

~~beetle~~   butterfly   lion   duck   jaguar
spider   parrot   tiger   toucan

Big cats	Birds	Insects
		beetle

1 Read and match.

1 100		one hundred thousand
2 500		ten thousand
3 1,000		one million
4 10,000		five hundred
5 100,000		one hundred
6 1,000,000		one thousand

2 Write the words.

1 80,000   *eighty thousand*

2 5,640 _____

3 15,648 _____

4 79,400 _____

5 181,979 _____

6 680,432 _____

7 360,000 _____

3 Read. Which continent has the longest rivers in total – Africa, North America, South America or Asia?

THE WORLD'S LONGEST RIVERS

AFRICA

The longest river in the world is in Africa. It's the Nile. Africa has three very long rivers. The Nile is about 6,600 km long, the Congo is about 4,700 km and the Niger, in western Africa, is about 4,200 km long.

THE AMERICAS

The longest rivers in South America are the Amazon and the Rio-Parana. The Amazon is about 6,400 km and the Rio-Parana is about 4,900 km long. The Mississippi-Missouri is the longest river in North America. It's about 6,200 km long.

ASIA

Asia has also got lots of long rivers. The Yangtze in China is about 6,300 km long, the Yellow River is about 5,400 km and the Lena in Russia is about 4,400 km long.

The River Nile

1 Read and complete the dialogue.

Matt	Do we have to be here at six?
Teacher	(1) ___No, you don't have to be here at six.___ The bus leaves at eight.
Andy	(2) _____ bring a tent?
Teacher	No, we have tents.
Lily	(3) _____ a rucksack?
Teacher	Yes, of course. You need a rucksack for your camera, an extra shirt and a snack.
Anna	Is (4) _____ all?
Teacher	No – don't forget your water bottle.
Rob	I haven't got a water bottle.
Teacher	Then you (5) _____ ask your parents to get you one.
Matt	So is there (6) _____ ?
Teacher	Yes. Don't wear boots, wear trainers, please.
Matt	All right.

2 🎧 007 Listen and say the words.

cheap   jeep

Phonics tip

Say *ch* and *j*. Can you hear that the *ch* sound is unvoiced but the *j* sound is voiced? That's the only difference!

3 Choose and write.

> bri~~dg~~e   da~~ng~~erous   ~~ma~~tch~~~   wat~~ch~~   gira~~ff~~e
> ~~j~~umper   langua~~g~~e   fri~~dg~~e   ~~ch~~ildren   ~~j~~am

1 Chelsea won the football _____**match**_____.
2 The jeep crossed the _____ to go over the river.
3 A _____ is a brown and yellow animal.
4 Let's _____ the children's channel on TV.
5 Two sweet foods are _____ and jelly.
6 Do you enjoy learning another _____?
7 Could you put the orange juice in the _____, please?
8 The _____ like Mr Church, their new teacher.
9 Put on your _____ or you'll catch a cold.
10 Don't touch that wire – it's _____!

4 🎧 008 Listen, check and say the sentences.

1 Match the sentence halves.

Language focus

1 You **have to** wear a big shirt — I'm a cool cat.

2 The jungle is dangerous, do you **have to** wear a hat?

3 When you walk through the jungle, with long sleeves.

4 I **don't have to**, and so are its leaves.

2 Look at the pictures and complete the sentences. ~~put up~~ brush collect make cook wash

1 First, _we had to put up the tent_____.

2 Then, _____.

3 After that, _____.

4 We _____.

5 Then _____.

6 Finally, _____ and then at last we went to sleep!

3 Think of things you had to do last weekend. Write sentences.

_____

_____

_____

_____

_____

1 Remember the story. Match the questions with the answers. There are two extra answers.

1 Why do the children follow the river? `d`
2 Why do the children climb the tree? ☐
3 Why do the children put their hands on their chests? ☐
4 Why does Alex give the old man a penknife? ☐
5 Why does the old man point to the fire? ☐
6 Why do the children climb the waterfall? ☐

a To hide from the jaguar.
b To make friends with him.
c To look for fruit.
d ~~To try to find a village.~~
e To show them where the food is.
f To show the man they are friendly.
g To make friends with the monkey.
h To get to the gate.

2 How do the children feel … ? (happy   scared   ~~hungry~~   nervous   excited)

1 **2** **3**

4 **5**

1 in the rainforest? _I think they feel hungry in the rainforest._
2 in the tree? _____
3 when they meet the man with the spear? _____
4 by the fire? _____
5 at the top of the waterfall? _____

3 Think and answer.

1 I feel happy _____.
2 I feel excited _____.
3 I feel scared _____.

4 Look and read. Match the text with the pictures.

When you meet people from different countries, remember that they might have different habits from you. Here are some things to know if you are in Thailand.

1 Thai people like to smile. They smile for many different reasons. When you meet someone from Thailand, a smile is always a good start. [d]

2 Don't shout. Thai people don't like to show when they are angry. If you want something, a smile always works better than getting angry. ☐

3 Never touch a Thai person on the head. It is very rude. ☐

4 Never show the bottom of your feet to people in Thailand. They think that the feet are the dirtiest part of the body. ☐

5 When you enter a house in Thailand, always take your shoes off and leave them outside the front door. ☐

6 The proper way to say 'hello' in Thailand is to do the 'wai'. Put your fingers together just below your face and lower your head. ☐

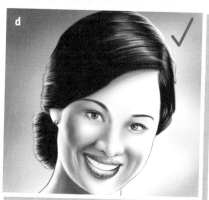

5 Complete the sentences about your country.

When you meet a new person …

1 you should _____.

2 you don't have to _____.

3 it's very rude to _____.

4 you should also remember to _____.

1 Look and read. Choose the correct words and write them on the lines. There are four extra words.

bottle

noise

fire

rainforest

mosquito

1	It's a plant and it hangs from trees. Monkeys use it for climbing.	creeper
2	It keeps us warm. You can cook on it.	
3	There are 13 of these in South America. Brazil is the biggest.	
4	Trees have a lot of these. Leaves grow on them.	
5	It's a big cat. It lives in South America.	
6	It's an insect and it bites. It isn't popular.	
7	There is water in it. You can swim in it.	
8	You speak one. English is one of them.	
9	It's a beautiful insect that can fly. It doesn't bite.	
10	You can carry water in it.	
11	They are reptiles. Some are poisonous.	

creeper

pool

countries

butterfly

frog

snakes

branches

jaguar

languages

sloth

009 Listen. Colour, draw and write.

Think and learn

1 Look and match the ecosystems with the photos.

1 desert   2 grassland   3 ~~ocean~~   4 rainforest   5 tundra   6 wetland

 a **3**    b    c    d    e    f

2 Write the names of the ecosystems from Activity 1 in the chart.

	Ecosystem	Climate	Plants	Animals
1	ocean	Cool or warm. Warmer on the surface. Can be very windy.	Plants that live in water – seaweed, seagrass, kelp, algae.	whale
2		Cold or hot. Rains all year. Lots of water.	Plants with long, strong roots that sit on water. Trees in water.	
3		Warm or hot. Rains a lot.	Lots of trees and creepers, many different plants.	
4		Hot. Dry for six months, wet for six months.	A few trees. Lots of grass.	
5		Very cold and windy. Snowy and icy but quite dry.	No trees. A few small plants.	
6		Hot or cold. Very dry.	No trees. Very few plants.	

3 Where do they live? Write the names of the animals in the chart in Activity 2.

 1    2    3    4    5   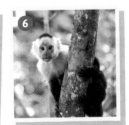 6

4 Read and answer.

Why do you think polar bears have white fur? How does it help them?

5 Why are rainforests important? Read and tick ☑ the reasons the article mentions.

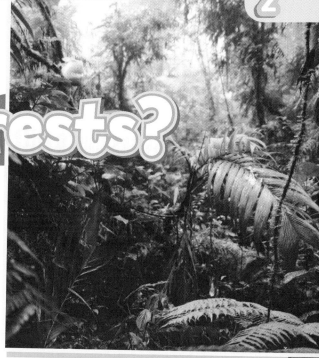

Why do we need rainforests?

Rainforests are amazing. More than 30 million different kinds of plants and animals live there. Many people live in rainforests too. Rainforests give them food, shelter and medicines. In fact, more than 25% of our medicines originally came from tropical rainforest plants.

Rainforests are sometimes called the 'lungs' of the Earth. The leaves on trees make energy from sunlight and a gas called carbon dioxide. This process makes a gas called oxygen. We need oxygen to stay alive. Carbon dioxide is dangerous for us if there is too much of it in the air. Trees help us by using up the dangerous gas and making the gas we need!

Rainforests are very important for the Earth's climate. The trees take water from the forest floor and put it back into the air as clouds. Scientists think that trees in the Amazon rainforest store more than half the Earth's rainwater.

The water in clouds can travel a long way before it falls as rain and ends up in rivers, lakes and oceans. It can even travel across continents, so water that starts as a cloud in Africa can fall as rain in the Americas! Rainforests help to recycle water and control the Earth's climate. Without them, the Earth would be much hotter and drier.

1 They make a lot of the food we eat. ☐

2 They have given some of our medicines. ☐

3 They make a gas we need to stay alive. ☐

4 They help to control the Earth's climate. ☐

5 They help to move water around the Earth. ☐

6 They give a lot of wood for furniture. ☐

6 ⭐ Project What have you found out about the ecosystem you chose? Complete the mind map.

```
                    ECOSYSTEM
        _____|_____
       |                |                |
     PLANTS          CLIMATE          ANIMALS
```

1 Correct the sentences by writing the missing word from the box in the right place.

~~to~~   thousand   had   don't   and   2012

1 You have wear a shirt with long sleeves.

<u>You have to wear a shirt with long sleeves.</u>

2 You have to cook the sausages. They are already cooked.

_____

3 When we arrived at the campsite, we to put up the tent.

_____

4 There are about ten kinds of birds in the world.

_____

5 In the Olympic Games were in London.

_____

6 There are three hundred sixty-five days in a year.

_____

2 Join the pieces to make words and use them to complete the sentences.

~~cree~~   ana   bee   bra   Slo   tun

conda   dra   nch   ~~per~~   tle   ths

1 The monkey grabbed the ____**creeper**____ and swung across the river.
2 There was a beautiful red bird sitting on the biggest _____ of the tree.
3 The _____ is an example of an ecosystem. It's very cold and windy.
4 A _____ is an insect with a hard, shiny back.
5 The _____ is the biggest snake in the Amazon forest.
6 _____ are animals that move very slowly and sleep a lot!

3 Complete the sentences with your own ideas.

1 Do we have to _____ to the party?
2 You don't have to _____. I bought some yesterday.
3 I have to _____. It's so hot.
4 She was really ill, so she had to _____.
5 Do I have to _____? I'm so tired.

What do I know?

1 **Read and tick** ✓**. Then write examples.**

1 I can use numbers from 100–1,000,000 correctly. ☐

Example with number: _____

Example with words: _____

2 I can use *have to* in the present and *had to* in the past. ☐

_____

_____

3 I can write the names of five things you can find in a rainforest. ☐

_____ _____ _____

_____ _____

2 🛡 **Write sentences to answer the Big Question.**

BIG QUESTION Why is the rainforest important?

_____

_____

_____

My diary

3 🛡 **Imagine you went on an expedition to the Amazon rainforest for a week. Write in your diary what happened.**

Think about: where you went.

where you spent the nights.

what you ate.

what you did all day.

_____

_____

_____

_____

_____

_____

_____

_____

3 The rock 'n' roll show

1 Look and write the names.

Davy Dee plays electric guitar in the band 4U.
Tony Scoot plays the bass guitar and Richie Fuzz
plays the drums. Lola and Cher are the backing
singers. Grace and Ruby are the dancers.
Buster Big is the bodyguard. Donna and Ruth are
their biggest fans.

1

Davy Dee

2

_____

3

_____

4

_____

5

_____

6

_____

7

_____

2 Read and complete.

Dear Emma,

Thank you for your birthday card. Guess what we
did for my birthday? Dad and I went to a rock
concert. Mum didn't go. She says rock concerts
are too loud for her. The band was called
The Dizzy Dodos. Miss D is the lead **(1)** singer
and there was another girl on the **(2)** d_____,
a boy with an **(3)** e_____ g_____ and a girl
with a **(4)** b_____ g_____. Dad and I were
close to the **(5)** s_____. It was really loud.
The **(6)** f_____ were screaming and some
wanted to climb on the **(7)** s_____, but the
(8) b_____ held them back.

We had lots of fun. Can you download The Dizzy
Dodos' album? Let me know what you think
of them.

Hugs

Lindsay

3 Imagine you are starting a band.
Think and write.

The name of the band:

_____

The instruments:

_____

_____

The names of the musicians:

_____

_____

_____

1 Complete the sentences with *going to* and the correct verb from the box.

take   play   sit

I'm **(1)** _____ a trick on him.

I'm **(2)** _____ and wait.

Look, he's **(3)** _____ a swim,

Oh, yummy, this tastes great!

2 Make questions for an interview with a rock star.

1 are / new / you / album / to / call / going / What / your / ?

What are you going to call your new album?

2 out / it / to / come / is / When / going / ?

_____

3 play / in London / Are / to / a concert / you / going / ?

_____

4 a holiday / you / the concert / have / going / to / Are / after / ?

_____

5 are / holidays / you / going / Where / your / to / spend / ?

_____

6 are / going / you / with / Who / take / you / to / ?

_____

3 What are they going to do at the weekend? Look and write sentences.

Tom's going to … _____ .

Daniel _____ .

Mia _____ .

Amy _____ .

4 What are you going to do at the weekend? Write sentences.

_____

_____

_____

1 🎧 **010** Listen to the song again and draw lines to link the words that rhyme. Write the groups of words.

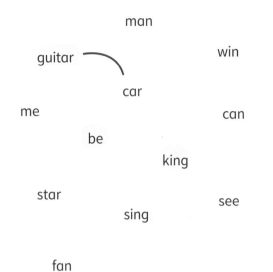

man

guitar

win

car

me

can

be

king

star

see

sing

fan

Group one	Group two
guitar	king
car	

Group three	Group four
me	fan

2 🎧 **011** Listen and say the words.

r**o**ck s**o**ck c**oa**t r**o**ll

3 Write the words in the s**o**ck or the c**oa**t.

~~rock~~ dr**o**p h**o**t d**o**g ~~roll~~ w**o**n't l**o**ng **o**ld l**o**st
gl**o**w b**o**ttle c**o**ld ag**o** s**o**rry f**o**rest expl**o**sion

Phonics tip

Listen carefully to hear the short sound in *rock* and *sock* and the long sound in *coat* and *roll*.

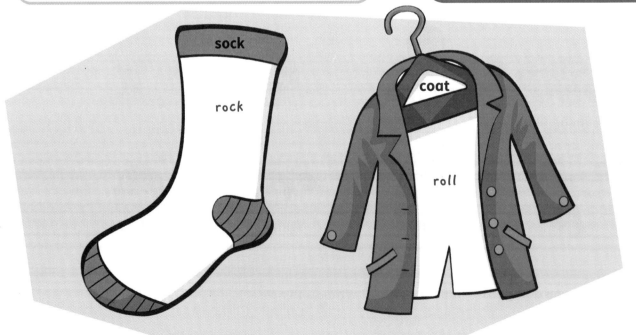

sock

rock

coat

roll

4 🎧 **012** Listen, check and say the words.

1 Read and write *past* or *to*.

1 It's five _____ seven.
Time to get up and go!

2 It's five _____ nine.
I'm hungry as a hippo.

2 Draw the times.

1 At eight o'clock, Mr Ferguson opened his shop.

2 You're late. It's already half past eleven.

3 At ten to nine, I was watching TV.

4 Please be at the meeting point at quarter to six.

5 'What's the time?' 'Five past twelve.'

6 She is going to arrive at quarter past seven.

3 Write the times.

1 It's five to eight.

2 _____

3 _____

4 _____

5 _____

6 _____

4 Look and write about parts of Harry's day.

Harry gets up at _____.

_____

_____

_____

1 Remember the story. Read and complete the text with words from the box.

wig ~~chat~~ shouting dressing room coat confused

We had a **(1)** _____chat_____ in the **(2)** _____ with Elvis. When we talked
about CDs, Elvis was very **(3)** _____. Then Elvis said, 'How am I going to
leave the theatre? I can already hear the fans **(4)** _____.' Alex had an idea.
He put on a long **(5)** _____, glasses and a **(6)** _____.

2 Read the summary and <u>underline</u>
seven more mistakes.

After the show they talk to Elvis.
Patrick tells Elvis that his <u>grandfather</u>
loves his music and has got all of his CDs.
Elvis is very happy, but a bit angry too.

Elvis invites the children to his house.
He tells them that being famous isn't always
fun. Sometimes he wants some peace and
quiet, but it's difficult with all his fans.
He doesn't know how to leave the theatre
without his fans seeing him. Alex thinks of a
plan. He sits on Patrick's shoulders and puts
on a hat and glasses. They wear a long coat
and leave the theatre. The fans are waiting
and screaming. They think Alex and Patrick
are Elvis. All the fans at the front of the
theatre run to see Elvis. Alex takes off his
disguise and the fans are sad. The boys get
into a helicopter. At the same time, the real
Elvis and Phoebe leave through the front
door. There are no fans waiting.

Back at his hotel, Elvis thanks the children
and they all eat pizza. Then the light
appears, and the children say goodbye and
walk through the gate.

3 Read and choose the best answer.

1 Why is Elvis happy when the children
  talk to him?
  a Because he likes talking to fans.
  b Because they call him 'king'.
2 Why is he confused that Patrick's
  grandmother likes him?
  a Because his fans are usually
    much younger.
  b Because he doesn't know what a CD is.
3 Why don't the fans follow Alex and
  Patrick's car?
  a Because they're not famous.
  b Because the car is too fast.
4 Why don't the boys want to go through
  the gate?
  a Because they are still eating.
  b Because they are having a good time.

4 **Read and draw the times on the clocks.**

Elvis gets up at twenty-five past nine.

Two hours later, he does a radio interview.

Forty-five minutes before he starts his show, he has a burger and milkshake.

The show starts at eight o'clock.

The show lasts for 95 minutes.

His journey to the hotel takes 25 minutes.

He watches TV for 80 minutes, then goes to bed.

5 **Read Elvis's answers and write the questions.**

1 **Alex** <u>Can you play the guitar?</u>
  Elvis Yes, I can play the guitar.

2 **Patrick** _____
  Elvis Yes, I always wanted to be a singer.

3 **Phoebe** _____
  Elvis My favourite singer is Chuck Berry. He's the best.

4 **Alex** _____
  Elvis I like action films.

5 **Patrick** _____
  Elvis No, I'm not married.

6 **Phoebe** _____
  Elvis Yes, of course you can have my autograph. Where do you want me to write it?

6 **Who's your favourite singer? Write five questions you would like to ask.**

Singer: _____

1 _____
2 _____
3 _____
4 _____
5 _____

1 Read and complete the dialogue. Choose from a–h.
You don't need to use all the answers.

1 Ben Lisa, you'll never guess what my grandpa got as a birthday present.

Lisa _Did he get a smartphone?_

2 Ben No, it's something from the 50s.

Lisa _____

3 Ben No, not a car. He got a jukebox.

Lisa _____

4 Ben It's a machine that plays music.

Lisa _____

5 Ben No, they didn't have CD players in the 50s. It plays old records.

Lisa _____

---

a So, it's a CD player, right?

b ~~Did he get a smartphone?~~

c Oh, those old round things. Great, I really want to see it.

d From the 50s? A guitar?

e A jukebox? What's that?

f No, you're right, I won't.

g So it's a drum kit, right?

h From the 50s? An old car?

---

2 🎧 **013** Listen and check your answers.

3 Read the email and write the missing words. Write one word on each line.

Dear Sarah,

1 We are back _____at_____ our hotel.

2 We _____ to see a very interesting exhibition with Grandpa and Grandma.

3 There _____ cars, chairs, tables, beds and lots of other things from the 50s.

4 Grandpa _____ photos of all the cars. I think he would really like to have one of those old cars.

5 Grandma wasn't very interested, _____ she loved the clothes exhibits. We both thought the swing skirts were fun!

6 I'll _____ you the photos when we're back in London.

Love

Emma

1 **Read and complete the sentences with words from the box.**

join   chance   loud   arranged   well   ~~nervous~~

1 Misha was _____ **nervous** _____ as she walked into the room.

2 'I would really like to _____ the band Girlz,' Misha told her best friend.

3 'I can't hear you. You're not _____ enough.'

4 Misha phoned her friend and _____ to meet her at the Golden Goose restaurant.

5 Misha had a second _____ when she went to meet Katia.

6 'You sing _____, but you don't look right,' Katia said to Misha.

2 What message can we learn from the story in the Student's Book? <u>Underline</u> the best summary.

a Don't give up on people.   **b** Don't listen to your dreams.   **c** Don't give up on your dreams.

3 Write a short advert for a band using the example to help you. Make up a name for the band.

WANTED
Electric Guitarist
for The

Metal Kings

We're going to be big!
Phone Mike on 970 234.

1 Look and match. What kind of music do you think they are playing?

orchestral music   jazz   rock music   hip hop

2 Read. <u>Underline</u> and correct the mistakes in the sentences below.

The birth of Jazz

Did you know that the word 'cool' comes from jazz and that jazz musicians invented the drum kit that many rock bands use today? Jazz started in the USA, around the beginning of the 20th century. It is a mixture of a kind of African American music called the 'blues' and European orchestral music. 'Blues' music comes from songs that African Americans used to sing while they were working in the fields. These were often sad songs. Rock 'n' roll music also comes originally from the 'blues'.

Common jazz instruments include drums, piano and guitar, as well as instruments that are also used in orchestral music, like saxophone and trumpet, and string instruments like the violin and double bass. Jazz musicians play from printed music, like orchestral musicians, but one big difference between orchestral music and jazz is that in jazz, the musicians sometimes make up the music as they go along. This is called improvisation.

1 <u>Orchestral</u> musicians invented the drum kit.

  Jazz musicians invented the drum kit.

2 Jazz is a mixture of hip hop and 'blues'.

3 'Blues' is often happy music.

4 The guitar, drums and harp are common jazz instruments.

5 The trumpet and violin are string instruments.

3 Read the article and complete the fact file.

LOUIS ARMSTRONG is one of the most famous jazz musicians. He was born in New Orleans, Louisiana, in the south of the USA, on 4th August 1901. He started playing the cornet – a wind instrument, like the trumpet – when he was 13. Later, in the 1920s, he changed to the trumpet. He is famous because he was very good at improvisation on the trumpet and he was a very good singer, with a strong, deep voice. His most famous song is *What a Wonderful World*, recorded in 1967. It became a best-selling record in the UK and many other countries around the world. At the time, Louis Armstrong became the oldest person to have a number one hit. He is so famous that the airport in New Orleans is named after him!

FACT FILE

Name: Louis Armstrong

Born (when): _____

Born (where): _____

Music genre: _____

Instrument: _____

Did he sing? _____

Famous record: _____

Famous because: _____

Fun fact: _____

4  Project What have you found out about the musician you chose?

Name:
Genre:
Fact 1:
Fact 2:

1 Make three sentences with the phrases in the diamond. Use three different phrases in each sentence.

1 I'm going to be there _____
   _____ .

2 _____
   _____ ?

3 _____
   _____ .

past nine

to the birthday party

a new camera

My sister

Are you

~~I'm going to be there~~

is going to buy

at five

going to come

2 Find the words and use them to complete the sentences.

1 j k x u b e o

2 g a i b k c n

3 g b d y r a d o u s

4 o h h i p p

5 g s o t p i l s h t

6 r r t c e l o a h s

1 My dad bought an old ____jukebox____, so he can play all his ancient records.

2 The singer was amazing and his _____ singers were great too.

3 When Jay-Z arrived, his _____ didn't allow people to get close to him.

4 In _____ music, rappers talk over the music.

5 When Elvis walked onto the stage, all the _____ were on him.

6 Mozart wrote a lot of _____ music.

3 Complete the sentences with your own ideas.

1 Next weekend, _____ .

2 Tomorrow, I'm not going to _____ .

3 In my next holidays, _____ .

4 Yesterday morning at ten to seven, _____ .

5 Tonight at ten to nine, _____ .

1 **Read and tick ✓. Then write examples.**

1 I can use *going to.* ☐

_____

2 I can use *past* and *to* the hour when telling the time. ☐

_____

_____

3 I can write the names of five things at a rock concert. ☐

_____ _____ _____

_____ _____

2 **Write sentences to answer the Big Question.**

BIG QUESTION What was music like in the past?

_____

_____

_____

3 **Look at the pictures. Imagine you play the electric guitar. Write the story.**

Think about: where you went.

what happened when you got there.

what you did.

how you felt.

_____

_____

_____

_____

_____

_____

_____

_____

4 Space restaurant

1 Look and write the words.

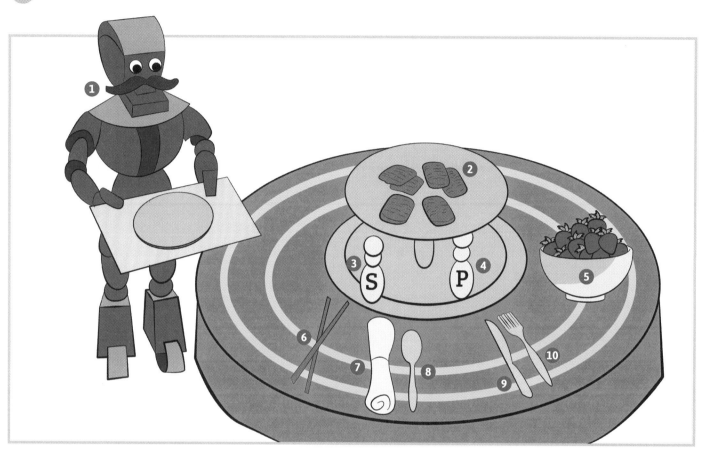

1	_____waiter_____	5	_____	9	_____
2	_____	6	_____	10	_____
3	_____	7	_____		
4	_____	8	_____		

2 Read and write the words from Activity 1.

1 This person asks you what you want to eat and drink. _____waiter_____

2 You wipe your mouth with it. _____

3 You eat soup with it. _____

4 You find it on the table. It's white. You mustn't eat a lot of it. _____

5 You hold these in one hand and use them to put food in your mouth. _____

6 You hold this in your hand and use it when you put food in your mouth. _____

7 You use it to cut your meat. _____

1 Read and complete. (a   the   This)

_____ year, _____ 1st (first) of May is _____ Monday.

2 Write sentences for the dates marked with a tick ✓.

OCTOBER			
1 ✓ Saturday	2 ✓ Sunday	3 Monday	4 Tuesday
5 Wednesday	6 ✓ Thursday	7 Friday	8 Saturday
9 Sunday	10 Monday	11 ✓ Tuesday	12 ✓ Wednesday
13 Thursday	14 Friday	15 Saturday	16 Sunday

14:10

1 The 1st of October is a Saturday.
2 _____
3 _____
4 _____
5 _____

3 🛡 Read. When is Oscar's birthday?

Tom and Amy are Oscar's brother and sister. Tom's birthday is on Wednesday the 15th of June. His sister's birthday is on the 1st of July, a Friday. Oscar's birthday is exactly between his brother's and his sister's birthday. What date is Oscar's birthday and what day is it on?

4 Read about Miguel. Look at his diary and write sentences.

Miguel Ganador loves his job. He eats in new restaurants and writes about them in newspapers. He doesn't often have to cook at home!

SEPTEMBER
① Saturday
② new French restaurant
③
④
⑤ new Turkish restaurant
⑥
⑦
⑧ new Egyptian restaurant
⑨
⑩
⑪
⑫
⑬ new Brazilian restaurant
⑭ new Italian restaurant

1 Miguel is going to eat in a new French restaurant on the 2nd of September. It's a Sunday.
2 _____
   _____
3 _____
   _____
4 _____
   _____
5 _____
   _____

1 Match the parts of the dialogue.

1 Today's the 6ᵗʰ of May!   [d]

2 Guess what I'm going to make tonight?   [ ]

3 I'm going to make your favourite meal.   [ ]

4 Yes. And ice cream – just how you like it.   [ ]

5 And that's not all. How about strawberry juice?   [ ]

a Strawberry juice – I can't wait!

b Awesome!

c What?

d ~~Yes, it is. It's my birthday!~~

e Chicken and chips? Cool!

2 Read and complete the dialogue with words from the box.

> Awesome   hungry   more   meal   ~~birthday~~   just   about   wait

Dad   Today's the 10ᵗʰ of August!

Lucy   Yes, it is. It's my (1) <u>birthday</u> .

Dad   Guess what I'm going to make tonight?

Lucy   What?

Dad   Your favourite (2) _____ .

Lucy   Sandwiches? Cool! Cheese and strawberry sandwiches with pepper?

Dad   Yes. And there's (3) _____ .

Lucy   Pizza ice cream?

Dad   Pizza ice cream – (4) _____ how you like it.

Lucy   (5) _____ !

Dad   And that's not all. To drink – how (6) _____ milk with salt?

Lucy   Milk with salt. I can't (7) _____ ! What time are we going to eat?

Dad   We? Well, I'm not really very (8) _____ . It's all for you!

3 **014** Listen and say the words.

<u>c</u>ity   <u>c</u>entre

Phonics tip

The letter *c* has the *s* sound before an *i* or an *e*!

4 Circle the *c* letters with an *s* sound.

Mmm … ice cream!

Ben was walking in the <u>c</u>ity when suddenly an alien stopped him. She said she was <u>c</u>alled <u>C</u>elia. It was her birthday and she asked Ben to <u>c</u>elebrate it with her. They <u>c</u>limbed inside her spa<u>c</u>eship. There was a <u>c</u>inema s<u>c</u>reen and a table with bowls of i<u>c</u>e <u>c</u>ream. Ben gave the alien his trading <u>c</u>ards. She said they were really <u>c</u>ool. They watched an ex<u>c</u>iting film about <u>c</u>rop <u>c</u>ircles. It was an ex<u>c</u>ellent party!

5 **015** Listen, check and say the words.

1 Complete the sentences with the correct form of the words.

> **Language focus**
>
> **1** If you _____ chocolate in the sun, it quickly _____ . (leave / melt)
>
> **2** If you _____ honey in tea, it _____ it sweet. (put / make).

2 Read and match.

1 If you want an apple, ☐   **a** you can have a dessert.

2 If you don't like the ice cream, ☐   **b** I can't get to sleep.

3 If you don't have a first course, ☐   **c** don't eat it.

4 If I eat too much, ☐   **d** you can take one from the kitchen.

3 Read and write the words in the correct form.

> go (x2)   rain   be (x4)   take   need (x3)   want (x2)   talk (x2)   ~~phone~~

1 If you _____**need**_____ help, please _____**phone**_____ me. You have got my number.

2 If you _____ happy, I _____ happy.

3 If the weather _____ fine, I _____ for long walks with the dog.

4 If it _____, I _____ my umbrella when I go out.

5 If you _____ to talk to someone, _____ to me now.

6 If I _____ some exercise, I _____ running in the forest.

7 If you _____ to learn the guitar, you _____ to practise every day.

8 If you _____ angry with Jack, _____ to him.

4 Complete the sentences.   feel sick   turns brown   heat up

If you eat too much chocolate, you _____ .

If you _____ water to a hundred degrees, it boils.

If there is no rain, the grass _____ .

1 🛡 **Remember the story. Read and complete the summary.**

The children waited **(1)** t _en_____ minutes for the first course. It was soup, but it was too **(2)** h_____ to eat with a spoon. The **(3)** w_____ told the children to throw it into the air. They did this and the soup broke into hundreds of little **(4)** b_____. They ate them with their chopsticks.

The second course was very strange. It was different coloured **(5)** s_____ which tasted of different things. You had to eat it very **(6)** q_____. The children got really excited by the last course. It was a type of **(7)** b_____ cake in the shape of a **(8)** s_____. It was made of **(9)** c_____ and there was **(10)** i_____ inside. The children ate lots of it. When the bill came, the children had to explain that they didn't have any **(11)** m_____. The waiter took them to the **(12)** k_____ to **(13)** w_____ the dishes. Luckily the **(14)** g_____ appeared and the children escaped.

2 **What did the children eat for each course? Look and order. Write *1*, *2* and *3*.**

a ☐   b ☐   c ☐

3 **Find the answers to the clues in the word search. Look → and ↓.**

1 The soup came in _____bowls_____.

2 The soup tasted like _____ and pepper.

3 The children ate the soup with _____.

4 The second course came in big _____.

5 There were lots of _____ on top of the spaceship.

6 You spend _____ at the restaurant.

7 The waiter gave the children the _____ at the end of the meal.

8 The cake was made of _____ and ice cream.

c	h	o	p	s	t	i	c	k	s
h	g	o	l	d	s	t	a	r	s
o	t	w	r	y	w	e	n	l	f
c	d	h	r	a	e	f	d	u	b
o	t	o	o	e	f	d	l	l	i
l	e	j	d	e	i	r	e	u	l
a	b	o	w	l	s	a	s	m	l
t	n	n	n	s	h	l	i	e	r
e	y	e	k	p	o	t	s	c	e

4 🛡 **What message can we learn from the story in the Student's Book? Underline the best summary.**

a If you want to buy something, make sure you have money.

b If you want to eat steam, it's easier to eat with chopsticks.

c If you put candles on a cake with ice cream, it melts.

5 Think of three ways for the children to pay the restaurant for their meal.

1 _____
2 _____
3 _____

6 Look at the pictures and find five differences.

Don't worry, Sir. It's dead.

Don't worry, Sir. It's dead.

1 In picture A, the man is wearing a napkin.
2 _____
3 _____
4 _____
5 _____

7 Put the sentences in order to make a story.

☐ The guest shouted.

☐ 'What's the problem?' the waiter asked.

☐ The guest showed the waiter an insect.

☐ The guest started to eat.

[1] The waiter served the tomato soup.

1 🎧 **016** **Listen and draw lines. There is one example.**

Robert David Betty

Katy Harry Helen

1 **Read the text. Choose the correct words and write them on the lines.**

EATING IN SPACE

Today, foods in space are similar to the foods we eat on Earth. On the International Space Station, there are more than 100 foods
1 on the _____ menu _____.
2 There are three meals a day, as well as _____ that can be eaten between meals.
3 Drinks include tea, coffee, fruit _____ and lemonade.
4 Salt and _____ are available too, but only as liquids. You might
5 need a lot of these, because food can _____ quite different in space. Some astronauts say it's really boring, so they have to use more spices and sauces.
6 What about _____? Do astronauts really eat ice cream in space? Well, they do, but not the dried type! They can eat normal ice cream, but only near the start of their space flight, while the freezer is working. After that, they're more likely to eat things like yoghurt
7 in any of the usual _____, like vanilla, strawberry or blueberry.
8 One thing's for sure – you need to hold on tight to your knife and _____ in space. If you don't, they float away!

1 plate ~~menu~~ café
2 meals desserts snacks
3 water sweets juice
4 pepper biscuits strawberries

5 taste lick invent
6 desserts sauces sweets
7 tastes flavours spices
8 chopstick bill fork

2 **Refer back to Student's Book page 53. What drink did you invent? What do you need and how do you make it?**

My invented drink: _____

Ingredients: _____

To make it …
1 _____
2 _____
3 _____

Think and learn

1 **Complete the sentences.**

> cacao   Lorries   pods   seeds   sun   ~~trees~~

1 Did you know that chocolate grows on _____**trees**_____ ?

2 The trees are called _____ trees.

3 Red, orange and yellow _____ grow on the trees.

4 The _____ inside each pod are called cocoa beans.

5 The beans taste sweeter after they have dried in the _____.

6 _____ take the dry beans to a chocolate factory.

2 **Read and answer.**

You can get white chocolate, milk chocolate and dark chocolate. Which do you think has the most cocoa? _____

3 **What do you need to make a pizza? Look and match.**

flour   water   yeast

①   ②   ③

④   ⑤   ⑥

oil   tomatoes   cheese

4 How is pizza is made? Look, read and match the instructions to the pictures.

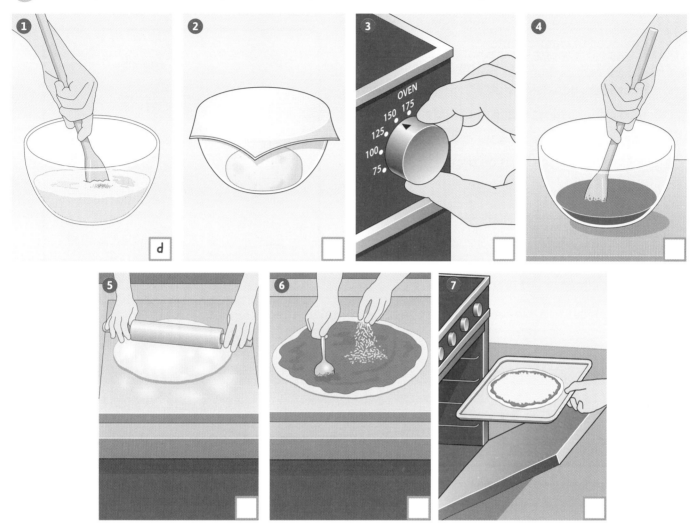

a Make your tomato sauce.

b Bake in the oven for 10–15 minutes.

c Roll out the bread mixture.

d ~~Mix the flour, water, oil and yeast to make the bread for the base.~~

e Heat the oven to 150˚C.

f Add your sauce and cheese.

g Leave the bread mixture in a warm place for 1–1.5 hours.

5 ⭐ Project What have you found out about the process of making jam in a factory? Write four things.

1 Choose six words or phrases to complete the sentences.

1 If _____it's_____ very cold, you need to wear a coat.

2 _____ too much salt in your soup, it tastes awful.

3 If you drop a glass bottle, the bottle _____ .

4 My brother's birthday is on the _____ June.

5 If you _____ chocolate, you feel sick.

6 It's Pam's _____ birthday on Sunday. Let's get her a card.

15th	opens
20th of the	21st of
If you put	breaks
gives me	eat too much
~~it's~~	eat too many

2 Join the pieces to make words and use them to complete the sentences.

chop   nap   pep   ~~straw~~   wai

~~berries~~   kin   per   sticks   ter

1 I love _____strawberries_____ – they're one of my favourite fruits.

2 We went to a Chinese restaurant and I learned how to eat with _____ .

3 Can you ask the _____ for a glass of water, please?

4 Don't put too much _____ in your soup.

5 You can use your _____ to wipe your mouth.

3 Complete the sentences with your own ideas.

1 If you eat _____ .

2 We're going to _____ in the summer.

3 I remember the _____ (date) because _____ .

4 If you don't like chocolate, _____ .

What do I know?

1 **Read and tick ☑. Then write examples.**

1 I can use ordinal numbers and write dates. ☐

Today is _____ .

My birthday is _____ .

2 I can write zero conditional sentences. ☐

If _____ .

If _____ .

3 I can write the names of five things in a restaurant. ☐

_____ _____ _____

_____ _____

2 **Write sentences to answer the Big Question.**

BIG QUESTION How is food prepared?

_____

_____

_____

My party

3 **Imagine it's a week before your birthday party. Write an invitation to your friends.**

Tell your friends: about the party. (When? Where? What time?)

what food you plan to eat. (Main course? Dessert? Drinks?)

what other plans you have. (Games? Music? Films?)

_____

_____

_____

_____

_____

_____

_____

5 The Wild West

1 Find nine words in the word search. Write them on the picture. Look → and ↓.

s	g	b	a	r	r	e	l	x	o
h	h	a	n	d	c	u	f	f	s
e	r	f	i	w	t	h	j	n	a
r	o	b	b	e	r	s	c	b	w
i	p	x	j	a	i	l	e	u	a
f	e	p	i	s	t	o	l	k	g
f	n	s	a	d	d	l	e	l	o
p	t	a	f	b	a	t	g	a	n

1 _____

2 sheriff

3 _____   4 _____

5 _____

6 _____

7 _____

8 _____   9 _____

2 Read and match.

1 The men look like   [e]   a looks around.

2 The people   [ ]   b look nervous.

3 The sheriff   [ ]   c the sheriff's pistol.

4 He looks as   [ ]   d there are the robbers!

5 She looks at   [ ]   e ~~trouble.~~

6 Look,   [ ]   f scared as her.

3 Look at the men in the picture and think of names for them.

Man on the left: _____

Man in the middle: _____

Man on the right: _____

1 Look and write the sentences.

1 **2** **3** **4** **5** **6**

1 It's made of plastic.   4 _____

2 _____   5 _____

3 _____   6 _____

2 Look and write the sentences.

1 **2** **3** **4** **5** **6**

1 It's used for opening nuts.   4 _____

2 They're used for opening doors.   5 _____

3 _____   6 _____

3 Read and circle the correct words.

Language focus

1 This cage is **made of** / **used for** metal.   3 These boots are **made of** / **used for** leather.

2 It's **made of** / **used for** catching me.   4 They're **made of** / **used for** drinking tea!

4 Draw an object and a pair/set of objects. Write sentences with *be made of* and *be used for*.

This _____.

It's _____.

These _____.

They're _____.

1 🎧 **017** Listen to the song again and complete the sentences.

1 Billie had *a silver gun and black and brown teeth.*

2 Billie was _____.

3 Billie robbed _____.

4 One day Billie _____.

5 Now Billie is _____.

2 🎧 **018** Listen and say the words.

rob – robber   sun – sunny   sit – sitting

Phonics tip

We double the consonant to show the first vowel sound is short.

3 Write and match. Don't forget to double the consonants.

clap   swim   ~~step~~   shop   stop   run

1 The friends _____**stepped**_____ into the yellow glow. **d**

2 The children went _____ for clothes.

3 The sheriff _____ the robber from escaping.

4 It's getting hotter. Let's go to the _____ pool.

5 Everyone _____ at the end of the play.

6 No _____, please! You must walk in the corridor.

Word watch

We don't double some consonants even when the vowel sound is short: *having*, *mixing*.

a

b

c

d

e

f Groovygear

4 🎧 **019** Listen, check and say the sentences.

1 **Complete the sentences.**

babies' baby's sheriff's robbers'

Language focus

1 I've got a ________________ badge.
2 They've got their ________________ badges.
3 Where's this ________________ hat?
4 They've got all the ________________ hats.

2 **Choose the correct word.**

1 **Amelias'** / **Amelia's** pony is six years old.
2 The **sheriffs** / **sheriffs'** badges are made of silver.
3 The **cowboys'** / **cowboys** horses are very fast.
4 **John's** / **Johns'** saddle is very heavy.
5 The **robbers** / **robbers'** scarves are black.
6 My **sister's** / **sisters** guinea pig is black and white.

3 **Rewrite the sentences.**

1 Her new jeans are green. (Susan)
Susan's new jeans are green.
2 His bike is broken. (Jack)
____
3 Her cat is called Snowy. (Mary)
____
4 Their favourite card game is called *Uno*. (the children)
____
5 *Wizard Race* is their favourite computer game. (my friends)
____
6 The water in their swimming pool is very cold. (my grandparents)
____

4 **Write sentences about the cars.**

Mum

Dad

Grandparents

Mum's car is new. ________________ ________________
________________ ________________ ________________

1 🛡 Remember the story. Read the summary and write the missing letters.

The children arrived in town in the middle of a **(1)** _b_ank robbery. They went and spoke to the sheriff. He told the **(2)** ch___ldren that the robbers were called the **(3)** Da___ton brothers and that there was nothing he could do because they were too dangerous. Patrick had a **(4)** p___an. While the brothers were doing the **(5)** robber___, he tied a rope around the legs of their horses. Alex also cut the **(6)** s___raps of their saddles. When the **(7)** brot___ers left the bank they saw the **(8)** rop___ around the legs and cut it off with a **(9)** ___nife. They got on their horses and rode away. When they jumped over a fence, the saddles came off and the robbers fell to the ground. The **(10)** sher___ff put **(11)** han___cuffs on them and put them in jail.

2 Write the missing letters from Activity 1 under the picture to find the name of a famous bank robber from the Wild West.

B _ _ _ _ _ _ _ _ _ _

3 Read and match.

1 The townspeople are worried because [f]   a the Daltons are too dangerous.

2 Phoebe is nervous because [ ]   b the children catch the Daltons.

3 The sheriff wasn't interested in the children's story because [ ]   c the sheriff gives them a badge.

d the children tricked them.

4 The children are scared because [ ]   e the Daltons have a big knife.

5 The sheriff is happy because [ ]   f ~~the Dalton brothers are in town.~~

6 The children are happy because [ ]   g the gate is glowing.

7 The Dalton brothers are angry because [ ]   h a robbery is going to happen.

8 Phoebe isn't scared because [ ]

4 Who do these things belong to? Write noun phrases.

1 The Dalton brothers' scarves.
2 _____
3 _____
4 _____
5 _____

5 🛡 **Read about the Dalton brothers and complete the chart.**

	Tim	Jim	Slim
Age	35		
Height			
Horse's name			
Banks robbed			

1 Slim is the youngest of the brothers. He is five years younger than Jim and eight years younger than Tim.

2 The oldest brother's horse is called Trigger.

3 The horse called Saddle belongs to the brother who is 27.

4 The horse called Pistol belongs to the tallest brother.

5 One of the brothers is 2 m, one is 1.75 m and one is 1.5 m.

6 The oldest brother is not the shortest brother.

7 Jim is taller than Slim.

8 The shortest of the brothers has robbed eight banks.

9 Jim has robbed nine banks.

10 One of the brothers has robbed three more banks than Jim.

6 🛡 **Read Phoebe's diary and complete. Use Activity 5 to help you.**

What an amazing day! The gate took us to the Wild West. We saw three men go into a bank. (We found out later they were the **(1)** ___Dalton___ brothers and they were very dangerous!) They were wearing **(2)** _____ to hide their faces. I told Alex and Patrick it was a **(3)** _____ and I was right. The boys had a plan. I told them to **(4)** _____ because the robbers were coming. The robbers came out and saw the boys. The tallest one, called **(5)** _____, had a big **(6)** _____. I was very scared. They jumped on their horses, called Trigger, Pistol and **(7)** _____, and rode away. Luckily the **(8)** _____ plan worked and the robbers fell off their horses. The **(9)** _____ put them in jail. When we were walking past the jail, the shortest one, whose name was **(10)** _____, shouted at us, but I wasn't scared. The gate was already glowing.

7 **Write a short diary entry for Alex or Patrick about the day.**

_____
_____
_____

1 🎧 020 **Listen and write.**

The Native American Museum

1 Expensive? Free for ___children under 15___

2 Where is it? Next to the _____

3 Open which days? From _____ to Wednesdays

4 Times? Opens _____ Closes 3 p.m.

5 Guided tours? Contact Mr _____

6 Phone number _____

2 **Look, read and write the missing letters.**

1 This is a __t__ e __e__ __p__ ee, a kind of tent used for living and sleeping in.

2 This is a traditional headdress from the __ iou __ tr __ b __.

3 __ i __ o __ skins were used for making clothes.

4 This is a modern house on a Native American __ e __ e ____ a __ io __.

1 Read and write the names next to the correct person.

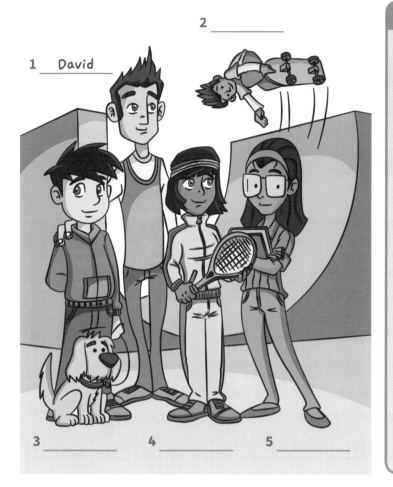

1 <u>David</u>

2 <u>   </u>

3 <u>   </u>   4 <u>   </u>   5 <u>   </u>

Dear Annie,

I recently read about how the Native Americans gave names to places and how these names meant something in their language. For example, Kansas means 'people of the south wind', Ohio means 'beautiful river' and Michigan means 'big lake'. I thought this sounded fun, so I decided to use the idea and do a 'translation' of some of my friends' names.

I've decided that David means 'boy of great height'. See how it works? Here are some more examples:

Ana – girl with a lot of energy

James – friend of the animals

Lucy – girl with windows in front of her eyes

Trevor – boy with wheels under his feet.

I had loads of fun doing this and I don't think I upset any of my friends. Have a go!

Love Beth

2 What can we learn about the Native Americans from their place names? <u>Underline</u> the best summary.

a They always lived next to water.

b Nature was important to them.

c They gave places the names of important people.

3 Write 'translations' for the names of some of your friends or people in your family.

Dad – man who likes news

Brother – boy who never asks before taking

1 What are they made of? Look and write.

wood   leather   animal bone   stone   ~~grass~~   glass beads

1

grass

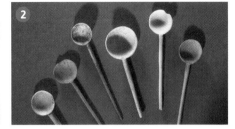

2

_____

3

_____

4

_____

5

_____

6

_____

2 Look and read about another material. Write *t* (true), *f* (false) or *ds* (doesn't say).

WHAT IS GOLD?

Gold is an expensive metal. If you are very lucky, you could find a small piece in a stream or even in your garden, but most gold is deep under the earth. You need to use special machines to dig it out. This is difficult and is one of the reasons why gold is so expensive. Gold is also expensive because it's very rare – that means there is not a lot of it.

What is gold used for?

- Because gold is expensive, it is used as money. All over the world, people want to buy gold.
- 60% of all the gold we have is made into jewellery. It is very soft and easy to work with. It is also very beautiful.
- Gold is often used in machines, like computers, because electricity can move through it easily.

1 Not all metals are found underground.   ds

2 Gold is sometimes found underwater.   _____

3 There is a lot of gold in the world.   _____

4 Gold is used in jewellery because it is strong.   _____

5 Electricity can't move through metals.   _____

3 Read the story and tick ✓ the best title.

On 24ᵗʰ January 1848, James Marshall was working on a farm in California, in the west of the USA, when he saw something shining in the water. He got down and picked a small piece of yellow metal out of the water. He showed it to his boss, a man called John Sutter, and both men agreed it was gold. Sutter was greedy and so he asked Marshall to keep it secret, but soon people began to hear about the discovery. When the news reached San Francisco, hundreds of men left their jobs and families to come and look for gold. They wanted to be rich and they were looking for adventure. This was the start of the great Californian gold rush. Over the next few years, people came from all over the USA to try to find a fortune. A few men found a lot of gold, but most went back home with nothing.

☐ The start of something big   ☐ A greedy man   ☐ The history of gold

4 Read again and answer.

1 Why didn't John Sutter want to tell anyone about the discovery?

_____

2 What kind of men joined the gold rush?

_____

3 Where else did people hear about the gold?

_____

4 Did all the men become rich?

_____

5 ⭐ Project What have you found out about Native American materials? Read and answer.

The material I chose was:	
Some things they made with this material were:	
They used this material because:	

History 67

1 Draw lines and complete the sentences with words from the box.

hobby   money   ~~made of~~   fighting   called   machines are used

1 The sheriff's gun is	to dig out the gold	Rex.
2 Pistols	_____ is	_____ .
3 Special _____	is used	and wood.
4 My parents'	_____ made of _____ metal	for _____ .
5 Our teacher's dog	are used for	cooking.
6 Gold	is _____	from the earth.

2 Find the words and use them to complete the sentences.

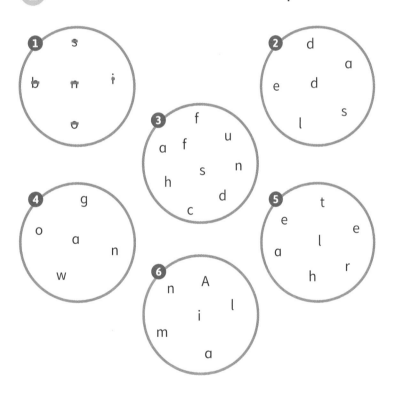

1 There used to be millions of
_____ bison _____ living in North
America. These days they are quite rare.

2 The sheriff put the _____
on his horse and rode away.

3 The sheriff got out his _____
and put them on the robber.

4 The horses stopped and three people got out
of the _____ .

5 Native American teepees were made of
_____ and wood.

6 _____ bones were used by
Native Americans to make flutes.

3 Complete the sentences with your own ideas.

1 _____ is made of _____ .

2 _____ are made of _____ .

3 _____ is used for _____ .

4 _____ are used for _____ .

5 My friend's _____ .

6 My parents' _____ .

What do I know? ①

Read and tick ☑. Then write examples.

1 I can write sentences with *made of* and *used for.* ☐

_____

_____

2 I can use possessive apostrophes. ☐

_____

_____

3 I can write the names of five things in the Wild West. ☐

_____ _____ _____

_____ _____

---

2 Write sentences to answer the Big Question.

BIG QUESTION — What was life like in the Wild West?

_____

_____

_____

My story ③

Look at the pictures. Imagine you are one of the people in picture 2. Write the story.

Think about: where you were.

what you saw.

what you did.

what happened next.

_____

_____

_____

_____

_____

_____

_____

_____

6 In Istanbul

1 Look and tick ✓ the correct picture.

1 carpet
ⓐ ⓑ
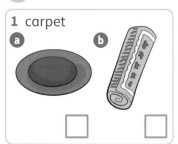
☐ ☐

2 cushion
ⓐ ⓑ
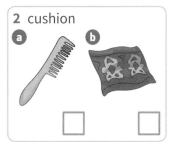
☐ ☐

3 earrings
ⓐ ⓑ

☐ ☐

4 basket
ⓐ ⓑ
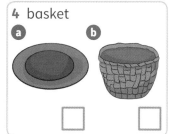
☐ ☐

5 cup and saucer
ⓐ ⓑ
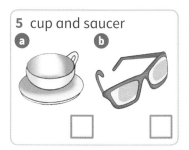
☐ ☐

6 soap
ⓐ ⓑ
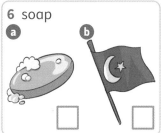
☐ ☐

7 comb
ⓐ ⓑ
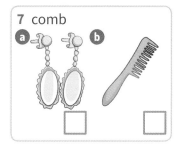
☐ ☐

8 sunglasses
ⓐ ⓑ
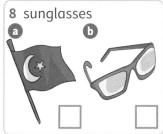
☐ ☐

2 Read and write the words from Activity 1.

1 You take it with you when you go to the market. You put things into it.
_____basket_____

2 It's on your breakfast table. You drink tea from it. _____

3 It's on the floor in the living room.
_____

4 You use it to wash your hands.
_____

5 You put it on a chair or sofa. _____

6 You wear them when the sun is shining.
_____

7 Jewellery that people wear in their ears.
_____

8 You use it to tidy your hair. _____

3 Read and complete the text with words from the box.

sea   because   world   Capital
most   river   bridge   Asia   ~~largest~~

www.tipsfortourists.com

Istanbul is one of the world's
(1) _____largest_____ and **(2)** _____
attractive cities. It is the only city in the
(3) _____ that is built on two
continents – Europe and **(4)** _____.
The continents are divided by a bit of the
(5) _____ that looks like a very big
(6) _____. It's called the Bosphorus
Strait. A long **(7)** _____ connects the
two continents. Tourists love Istanbul
(8) _____ it offers a mixture of
Western and Eastern traditions. In 2010, Istanbul
became the European **(9)** _____
of Culture.

1 Look and write *should* or *shouldn't*.

Language focus

1 When you come to my jungle, there are things you ✔ _____ try.
2 When you come to my jungle, there are things you ✘ _____ do.

2 Read and match.

1 My feet hurt. I can't walk. [c]
2 It's raining outside. [ ]
3 My hand hurts. [ ]
4 One of my teeth hurts. [ ]
5 The dog isn't in the house. [ ]

a You should take your umbrella.
b You should see a dentist.
c ~~You should wear comfortable shoes.~~
d You shouldn't leave the door open all the time.
e You shouldn't play computer games all day!

3 Write sentences using *should* or *shouldn't*.

He shouldn't take photos .

They _____
_____ .

She _____
_____ .

He _____
_____ .

She _____
_____ .

They _____
_____ .

1 🛡 **Look, read and answer. Which is more expensive? Tick a, b or c.**

ⓐ
1 mug
1 pair of sunglasses ☐

ⓑ
1 book
1 pair of sunglasses ☐

ⓒ
1 mug
1 book ☐

2 **A brother and sister are looking for a present for their father. Write a dialogue.**

Girl (Suggests buying Dad a present.) **(1)** Let's get Dad a present. _____

Boy Why? (Asks if it is his birthday.) **(2)** _____

Girl No! Because it's Father's Day!

Boy Ah. OK. (Agrees with suggestion to buy present.) **(3)** _____

Girl (Suggests a book.) **(4)** _____

Boy (Asks how much it is.) **(5)** _____

Girl (Tells him the price.) **(6)** _____

Boy (Says it's expensive.) **(7)** _____

Girl (Suggests sunglasses instead.) **(8)** _____

Boy (Agrees.) **(9)** _____. They're much funnier than Dad's jokes!

3 🎧 021 **Listen and say the words.**

<u>s</u>ugar   sta<u>t</u>ue

Phonics tip

The *sh* and *ch* sounds are sometimes spelled in different ways.

4 **Read. Write the underlined words in the chart.**

The <u>ch</u>ildren went to a <u>sh</u>op to buy a present for their tea<u>ch</u>er. Everything was too expensive, so they went to a <u>ch</u>eaper shop between the <u>ch</u>urch and the train sta<u>t</u>ion. They saw a ma<u>ch</u>ine whi<u>ch</u> made tiny sta<u>t</u>ues out of <u>s</u>ugar. The girls were <u>s</u>ure that Miss Saunders would like su<u>ch</u> a spe<u>c</u>ial machine!

sh sounds	shop,
ch sounds	children,

5 🎧 022 **Listen, check and say the words.**

1 Complete the sentences. [all right   Could   course   mind]

Language focus

Do you **(1)** _____ if I ask you a question?   Not at all.

Could you show me the way to the lake, please?   Yes, of **(2)** _____.

Could you help me carry my bag?   Yes, **(3)** _____.

(4) _____ I take a selfie, please?   OK. Say 'Cheese!'

2 Put the dialogue in the correct order.

☐	**Customer**	Not at all. What do you want to ask?
☐	**Customer**	Buy? Oh no, but I like trying things on.
☐	**Customer**	Could I also try the silver ring on?
☐	**Customer**	The earrings and the silver ring look great.
1	**Customer**	Do you mind if I try on the earrings?
☐	**Assistant**	Are you going to buy anything?
☐	**Assistant**	Those earrings? Not at all.
☐	**Assistant**	The silver ring? Of course.
☐	**Assistant**	Yes, they do. They're lovely on you. Do you mind if I ask you a question?

3 Make questions.

1 I / another / of / Could / piece / have / cake / ? <u>Could I have another piece of cake?</u>

2 look / Could / book / that / have / I / a / please / at / over there, / ? _____

3 Could / explain / Maths / to / you / homework / the / me, / please / ? _____

4 the / you / Could / tell / me / please / time, / ? _____

4 Write questions. Use the words from the box.   [close   ~~give~~   try on   sit]

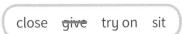

❶ ❷ ❸ ❹

<u>Do you mind if I give</u> _____   _____   _____
<u>your dog a sandwich?</u> _____   _____   _____

1 Write the names of the places under the photos.

1 _____ 2 _____ 3 _____

2 Remember the story. Read the summary. Write the sentence numbers in the boxes.

1 They don't find Phoebe anywhere.

2 It is very busy.

3 ~~They make a list of all the places they want to go.~~

4 They think this is the best way to find Phoebe.

The children are in Istanbul in Turkey. They get a guidebook from the tourist office and sit down to read it. [3] Phoebe is very excited and wants to go sightseeing. They decide to take the underground and go to Taksim station. [ ] The boys get on the train, but Phoebe is too slow and she gets left behind. The boys decide to go to all the places they wanted to visit. [ ] They go to the Blue Mosque, the Bosphorus Bridge and the Spice Market. [ ] They meet a Turkish boy called Ali. He says they should go back to Taksim station. They all go there and find Phoebe. Ali invites Phoebe to see the sights with him the next day, but Phoebe says she can't. She can see the gate glowing at the top of the escalator.

3 Who is speaking? Write the names.

1 'Have you got a guidebook about the city?' ___Phoebe___

2 'Hurry up, Phoebe.' _____

3 'Oh no. The train's leaving without me.' _____

4 'That's a good idea. She'll definitely be at one of them.' _____

5 'We're looking for our friend.'
_____

6 'Can I come with you?' _____

7 'But thank you for the invitation.'
_____

8 'Where did they go?' _____

4   **Look at the photos of famous places. Write two sentences about each one. Use the phrases below or your own ideas.**

It's amazing!   That's so cool.   I'd love to go there.   What a wonderful place.   I'd love to take a photo.

The Iguazu Falls in Brazil and Argentina

The Burj Khalifa in Dubai

The Taj Mahal in India

Mount Bromo in Indonesia

1 They're beautiful. I'd love to go there.

2 _____

3 _____

4 _____

5 **Read the postcards. Which of the places in Activity 4 are Allan and Amy visiting?**

Dear Jessica,

What an amazing place! There's so much water. And the noise! It's so loud. It's a really beautiful place too. There are lots of trees and birds. You would love it here. I've got you a souvenir. It's a cap with a picture of a toucan on it. I hope you like it.

See you,

Allan

Dear Thomas,

Isn't it wonderful? It's made of white stone, but now the sun is going down and it looks pink. Amazing! Mum is taking a photo of the wonderful building and the pool in front of it. The water of the pool is like a mirror where you can see the whole building. I'll show you when we get home.

Love Amy

5 Daisy Avenue

Oxford

OX52 2ZFS

1 _____

2 _____

1 🎧 023 What did each person in Mrs Salt's family buy in the souvenir shop? Listen and write the letter. There is one example.

Mrs Salt ☐

Daisy **b**

Anna ☐

John ☐

Katy ☐

a Istanbul's a dream!

b Sights and Sounds of Istanbul

c Hamit Anltintop   Hakan Sukur   Tuncay   Rustu Recber

d

e Ice Maiden

f

g

h Coffee

2 Choose two more souvenirs from Activity 1 and write a sentence about each one.

1 Mrs Salt bought a set of beautiful glass cups and saucers.

2 _____

3 _____

1 **Read the conversation and choose the best answer. Write a letter (A–H) for each answer.
You do not need to use all of the letters.**

Peter It's Nick's birthday on Monday.
We should go out for dinner.

Tim <u>G</u>

Peter I'm not sure. Have you got any ideas?

Tim __

Peter He doesn't really like spicy food.

Tim __

Peter Are you sure?

Tim __

Peter OK then, I'm sure he'd like that!
Which one?

Tim __

A Hmm … OK. How about an Italian
restaurant? He loves pizza.

B Yes, my father works in the city.

C I've got an idea. Let's ask him!

D I'm sure it's Friday. After school.

E Yes, I am. He told me last week.

F That's a great idea.

G ~~Good idea, but where should we go?~~

H Well, we could try the new Indian
restaurant in town.

2 🛡 **Where are the foods from? Read and write the foods in the correct place.**

Can you imagine life without chocolate? Or tomatoes for your pizza? Can you imagine walking down the street and not seeing any coffee shops? Today, different types of food are grown, sold and eaten in many places around the world. But that wasn't always the case.

Before the 1500s, there were many foods that only existed in Europe and Asia or the Americas.

That all changed when European explorers travelled to South and Central America in the 15ᵗʰ and 16ᵗʰ centuries. They took wheat, and fruit, like oranges and lemons, from Europe to the Americas. In exchange they brought back tomatoes, pineapples, potatoes and corn.

Europeans also introduced South American people to bananas and coffee, which first came from Africa, and sugar and rice, from Asia. But, did you know that chillies, which are very important in Asian cooking, first came from South America? And, of course, so did chocolate!

From Europe	From South America	From Asia or Africa
wheat		

1 **Read and match.**

pieces of glass and stone   mosaic   surface

_____   _____   _____

A mosaic is a special kind of art where a surface is covered by small pieces of coloured glass or stone. The pieces – or 'tiles' – are placed carefully and stuck together tightly. They can make amazing designs and pictures.

2 **Look and read. Write _t_ (true), _f_ (false) or _ds_ (doesn't say).**

MOSAICS
fascinating facts!

Mosaics have been found from many different times and in many different countries.

- Some of the earliest known mosaics are from Western Asia. They are over 4,000 years old.
- The two biggest mosaic museums in the world are in Turkey.
- Mosaics were very popular in Roman times. They were strong, easy to clean and waterproof, so the Romans often used them on the floors of big buildings.
- One of the most famous mosaic artists in the 20th century was Antoni Gaudí, from Barcelona in Spain. His mosaics can be seen all over the city – on houses, big buildings and in parks. Mosaic souvenirs are very popular in Barcelona!
- The biggest mosaic in the world today is on a wall in Hanoi, Vietnam. It is around 6.5 km long. It is made of stone tiles from a local village.
- A French street artist, known as Invader, has become famous for his mosaics on walls in cities all over the world. They show characters from 1970s video games!

1 You can see mosaics all over Istanbul.   _ds_
2 The biggest mosaic in the world today is in Turkey.   _____
3 In Roman times, mosaics were very useful.   _____
4 You have to go to a museum to see Gaudí's mosaics.   _____
5 The mosaic in Vietnam is made of materials from near Hanoi. _____
6 You can see Invader's work in Paris.   _____

3 Look, read and number the pictures.

Although traditional mosaics are made with glass or stone tiles, you can make your own using paper. Just follow these simple steps:

1 Draw some ideas for your design.

2 Choose your favourite design and copy it onto a piece of white card.

3 Take some sheets of paper in different colours.

4 Cut the paper into small pieces to make your 'tiles'.

5 Stick your paper 'tiles' onto your design. Leave a little white space between the 'tiles'.

6 You have a finished mosaic!

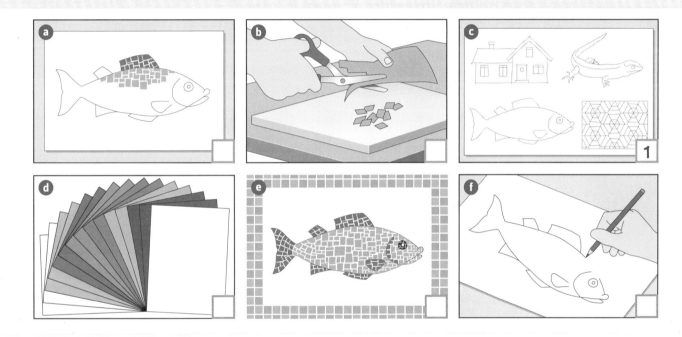

4 Look. What do you think the mosaic will show?

5 Colour and check. Was your prediction right?

6 **Project** Follow the instructions in Activity 3 to make your own paper mosaic.

Key

1 brown   **4** red

2 blue   **5** yellow

3 grey

1 Correct the sentences by writing the missing word from the box in the right place.

help   try   sure   ~~have~~   shouldn't   mind

1 Could I a cheese sandwich, please?

Could I have a cheese sandwich, please?

2 Do you if I use your sunglasses?

_____

3 You worry that you forgot your cap. Use one of mine.

_____

4 Make that you bring a coat. It's cold at the moment.

_____

5 Could you come over and me for a moment, please?

_____

6 You should to remember these words. They are very useful.

_____

2 Join the pieces to make words and use them to complete the sentences.

bas   car   ~~cush~~   mos   sau

aic   cer   pet   ~~ions~~   ket

1 The _____cushions_____ on the sofa are really soft and comfortable.

2 My aunt bought my mum a beautiful cup and _____ for her birthday.

3 I'm terribly sorry. I made some marks on your _____ with my shoes.

4 There was a long _____ on the wall of the station.

5 Put the cheese, the bread and the apples into the _____ . We'll have a picnic.

3 Complete the sentences with your own ideas.

1 In the classroom, you shouldn't _____.

2 You should _____ when you are bored.

3 I'm hungry. Could I _____?

4 I'm a bit hot. Do you mind _____?

What do I know?

1 **Read and tick ✓. Then write examples.**

1 I can write sentences with *should* and *shouldn't*. ☐

_____

_____

2 I can write questions with *Could I … ?* and *Do you mind if I … ?* ☐

_____

_____

3 I can write the names of five types of souvenirs. ☐

_____ _____ _____

_____ _____

2 **Write sentences to answer the Big Question.** **BIG QUESTION** What can we buy in different countries?

_____

_____

_____

My email

3 **Imagine your friends don't know what to do for their holiday. Write an email to give them advice.**

Think about: where they should go.

what they should take.

what they should and shouldn't do there.

_____

_____

_____

_____

_____

_____

_____

_____

7 The story teller

1 Read and complete the text.

Shakespeare was one of the greatest writers of all times. Even today, theatres all over the world put his

plays on stage. In Shakespeare's time, there were only male (1) ____actors____ . When they

acted women's roles, they wore a (2) _____ and women's (3) _____ .

And when they played men's roles, they didn't wear trousers, they wore (4) _____ .

The actors sometimes wore a (5) _____ too. In Shakespeare's time, most of the

(6) _____ stood. They talked, ate and shouted when they didn't like what they saw.

2 Use a verb from box A and a noun from box B to complete the sentences.

A
| wear   be   stand up |
| gets   ~~light~~   plays |

B
| Audiences   ~~candle~~   actor |
| tights   lute   mask |

1 Can you ____light____ a ____candle____ , please? It's getting a bit dark in here.
2 Many superheroes _____ a _____ , so no-one can see their face.
3 When I grow up, I want to _____ an _____ .
4 _____ often _____ and clap when they really like a show.
5 My gran _____ the _____ in our school plays.
6 Mum gets cross when she _____ a hole in her _____ .

3 Write the words in the correct column.

| ~~earrings~~ costume jail sheriff |
| robber tights tourist office museum |
| waiter necklace cowboy wig vet |
| train driver underground station mask |
| bridge theatre |

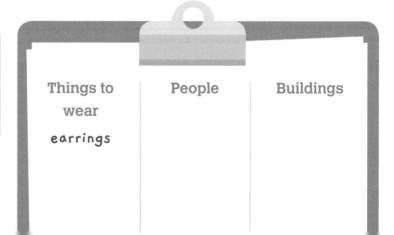

Things to wear	People	Buildings
earrings		

1 Match the sentence halves.

Language focus

1 Why don't we do a jungle show   to join in too and bring his friends along.

2 Great idea! I'll build   the monkeys to sing a funny song.

3 And then I'll get   for everyone to see?

4 We'll ask the snake   a stage right there by the tree.

2 Look and write the sentences.

~~bake~~   buy   cook   drive   help   repair

Girl It's Lea's birthday.
Boy I'll bake a cake for her.

Boy I'm hungry.
Mum _____

Boy I'm tired.
Girl _____

Girl The bus didn't come. I'm late.
Dad _____

Boy I really like that cap.
Mum _____

Girl My bike is broken.
Boy _____

3 Your parents ask you to help in the house. Write three things you'll do.

1 _____

_____

2 _____

_____

3 _____

_____

1 🎧 **024** **Listen to the song again and complete the sentences.**

poem   rocket   secret   song

1 I'll write you a _____.

2 I'll tell you a _____.

3 I'll sing you a _____.

4 I'll build you a _____.

2 **Write the rhyming pairs. Find one more rhyme for each pair.**

~~zoo~~   hat   things   all   ~~you~~   buy   take   make   rings   small   cat   fly

1 ___zoo___ / ___you___   ___two___   **4** _____ / _____   _____

2 _____ / _____   _____   **5** _____ / _____   _____

3 _____ / _____   _____   **6** _____ / _____   _____

3 🎧 **025** **Listen and say the words.**

little   mouse

Phonics tip

Sometimes an *e* at the end of a word is silent. It doesn't change the pronunciation of the rest of the word.

4 **Complete the words with the endings from the box. Match the sentences with pictures a–f. The endings can be used more than once.**

ce   le   re   se   de   ge

1 There's a hor _se_ in the hou____.   `d`

2 The audien____ watched the play in the theat____.   ☐

3 Can you blow out that cand____ on the tab____?   ☐

4 I like that neckla____ with the purp____ stone in it.   ☐

5 The girl with blon____ hair is in the midd____.   ☐

6 How many peop____ live in this villa____?   ☐

5 🎧 **026** **Listen, check and say the sentences.**

Song practice; phonics focus: silent *e*

1 Complete the sentences with the present perfect of the correct verb. drop   hear   shout   fall

Language focus

1 I've just _____ the explorer. Listen!
2 He's just _____ over a tree. Look!
3 They've just _____ some nuts on him.
4 He's just _____ at them. See?

2 Read and match.

1 My hands are clean. `e`
2 They're not hungry.
3 Their car is really clean.
4 My mum's happy with me.
5 I'm tired.
6 Bill and Jane are not at home.

a They've just had a big breakfast.
b I've just tidied my room.
c I've just walked 15 kilometres.
d They've just gone to the park.
e ~~I've just washed them.~~
f I've just washed it for them.

3 Read and complete the sentences.

1 Don't make a mess in the kitchen – I **'ve** just ___cleaned___ it. (clean)
2 I ___ just _____ some really good news. (hear)
3 We can't buy that book for Ellie's birthday – she _____ just _____ it. (read)
4 Paul _____ just _____ – he was really tired. (get up)
5 He _____ just _____ his arm. Get a plaster, please. (cut)
6 The baby _____ just _____ his first word. (say)
7 I ___ just _____ your favourite cup – sorry, Mum. (drop)
8 Sorry, Mia isn't in. She _____ just _____ for the supermarket. (leave)

4 Look and write sentences.

He's just jumped in the swimming pool.

_____

_____

1 Remember the story. Write the letters (A–E) to complete the summary.

The children are at the theatre, watching William Shakespeare and his new play.
(1) _E_ At the end, the children go and talk to Shakespeare. **(2)**___ Patrick trips one of the men up with a sword and he chases the rest of them away. **(3)**___ There is a knock at the door. **(4)**___ This time, Shakespeare saves the children. **(5)**___ As the children walk on stage to join Shakespeare, the gate appears and they disappear.

A Shakespeare changes the end of the play and it is a big success.

B Just then, some angry men come onto the stage and start shouting.

C It is the men again and they are still very angry.

D The children go to Shakespeare's house and tell him to change the end of the play.

E ~~The audience don't like the play and ask for their money back.~~

2 Read and choose the best answer.

1 The children talk to Shakespeare because …

(a) he looks sad.

b they want to meet a famous person.

c he is on his own.

2 Shakespeare invites the children to dinner because …

a they are hungry.

b he wants to hear their ideas.

c he wants to thank them for their help.

3 The children tell Shakespeare to make his play …

a happier.

b sadder.

c shorter.

4 The men come to Shakespeare's house to get …

a Alex.

b Patrick.

c Shakespeare.

5 Shakespeare stops the trouble by …

a telling the men that his play has a new ending.

b offering the men cheap tickets.

c calling the police.

3 How do these items appear in the story? Write sentences.

1 Alex and Patrick hide behind the box.

2 _____

_____

3 _____

_____

4 How many words of four letters and more can you make from the letters in the name SHAKESPEARE?

press _____ _____ _____ _____ _____

5 Read the dialogue and use it to complete the ticket.

Billy I've just got a ticket to see Shakespeare's *King Lear*.

Julia Really? Where is it on?

Billy It's at the Little Theatre in Bridge Street.

Julia And what day are you going to see it?

Billy I'm going on Monday 8th June.

Julia What time does it start?

Billy 8 p.m.

Julia Have you got good seats?

Billy I think so. I'm in row B, seat number 24. I hope that's at the front.

Julia And how much did it cost?

Billy €12.

Julia I think I'll go too.

Billy Well, you should hurry up. The tickets are selling fast.

The (1) _Little_ Theatre proudly presents:

Shakespeare's (2) _____

Monday (3) _____

Time (4) _____

Seat number (5) _____

€ (6) _____

6 Complete the ticket with your own ideas. Then write a short dialogue.

THE _____ THEATRE
proudly presents:

Shakespeare's
Romeo and Juliet

Day _____

Time _____

Seat number _____

€_____

A I've just got a ticket to see Romeo and Juliet.

B Really? Where is it on?

_____
_____
_____
_____
_____
_____
_____
_____
_____

7 Have you ever been to the theatre? If so, what did you see? If not, what would you like to see?

_____
_____

1 Read the text. Choose the correct words and write them on the lines.

William Shakespeare
is possibly the BEST-SELLING fiction author of all time!

1   He _____was_____ born in Stratford-upon-Avon, in England –

2   probably _____ 23rd April 1564, although the exact date is a mystery!

When he was 18 years old, William married Anne Hathaway,

3   and they _____ three children – two girls and

4   _____ boy. We don't know much about Shakespeare's

5   life in his 20s, but when he was 30, the family moved _____ London.

He worked as an actor, and then started writing plays and poems.

6   His plays were often very funny _____ he used words very cleverly.

7   He invented more _____ 1,000 words that we still use in the English language today!

8   Although his plays were very popular at the time, _____ published them

9   until after he died. _____, people read and perform them all over the world.

10 Perhaps they are _____ popular because they are about themes that everyone

can understand – love, family relationships, power and fear of dying.

1 were	~~was~~	is
2 on	in	at
3 did have	have	had
4 a	some	the
5 in	to	at
6 but	so	because
7 about	than	of
8 no-one	someone	anyone
9 Tomorrow	Yesterday	Today
10 such	so	so much

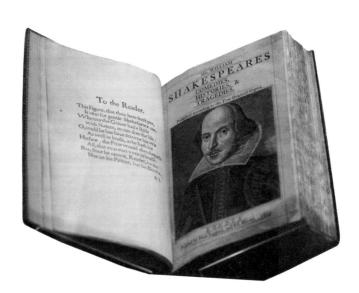

1 🎧 **027** Who said or thought it? Listen and tick ✓.

1	Marlowe's wife ☐	Barney ☐	Marlowe ☐
2	Barney ☐	One of the men ☐	Marlowe's wife ☐
3	Marlowe's wife ☐	Marlowe ☐	The three men ☐
4	Marlowe ☐	Marlowe's wife ☐	Barney ☐
5	Barney ☐	The three men ☐	Marlowe's wife ☐
6	One of the men ☐	Marlowe's wife ☐	Marlowe ☐

2 What message can we learn from the story in the Student's Book? Underline the best summary.

a It's always best to be honest.

b Being clever is more important than being honest.

c If you're clever, you don't need to be honest.

3 Look at the pictures to help you write the ending of the story.

_____
_____
_____
_____
_____
_____
_____
_____
_____
_____
_____
_____

Think and learn

1 **Read and complete the sentences.**

> ~~characters~~ comedies history plays
> make-up props special effects tragedies

1 The ___characters___ are the people that the play is about.

2 The _____ are the objects that actors use when they are in a play.

3 Actors sometimes use _____ on their faces so that they look more like the characters.

4 In the theatre, _____ can be created by using lights or sounds.

5 Shakespeare wrote ten _____. They were all about kings of England.

6 Shakespeare's _____ are quite serious plays. Often something sad or bad happens.

7 Lots of funny things happen in Shakespeare's _____ and they can be quite confusing!

2 **History, comedy or tragedy? Read about six of Shakespeare's plays and complete the chart.**

Richard III Richard of Gloucester is the King's younger brother. He wants to be king. He will do anything to become king himself and doesn't always tell the truth.

The Tempest After a fight with his brother, Antonio, Prospero goes to live on an island. When Antonio's ship has an accident at sea, he arrives on the same island. Antonio's son wants to marry Prospero's daughter. After a party and some magic, everyone is friends again.

Twelfth Night Viola and Sebastian are twins. Viola dresses as a boy to get a job with the Duke. The Duke's daughter believes she is a boy and wants to marry her! There are lots of jokes and confusion.

Macbeth Macbeth sees some women who tell him he will be king. His wife tells him to kill the King. He does, but he is afraid that other people will find out, so he kills them too. He and his wife both become mad because they feel so bad.

Hamlet Hamlet's father dies. His mother marries his uncle. He sees his father's ghost and wants to find out the truth. There is a lot of fighting. Many people die, including Hamlet.

Henry V The action takes place in the 15th century. Henry V is the King of England. He is at war with France, but eventually makes peace – and marries a French princess!

HISTORY	TRAGEDY	COMEDY
Richard III		

90 History

3 Read about the six Shakespeare plays again and write a name.

Who …

1 has a twin sister?   Sebastian

2 is told he will become king?   _____

3 isn't always honest?   _____

4 marries someone from a different country?   _____

5 sees a ghost?   _____

6 goes to live on an island?   _____

4 ⭐ Project Read and complete the mind map about your project.

Props:
_____
_____
_____

Costume:
_____
_____

Character:
_____

Character:
_____

Costume:
_____
_____
_____

Kind of play:
_____
_____
_____

Props:
_____
_____

Props:
_____
_____
_____

Character:
_____

Costume:
_____
_____
_____

5 ⭐ Project Write a short description of your theatre stage.

_____

_____

_____

1 Make three sentences with the phrases in the diamond.
Use three different phrases in each sentence.

1 Our class _____

_____ .

2 _____

_____ .

3 _____

_____ .

We'll ask

has just won

I will

Our class

Mum if we can

a match against class 5C

with your homework

have a party on Saturday

help you

2 Find the words and use them to complete the sentences.

1 e e o m s t u

2 e d m o y c

3 i d e e c u n a

4 s t a h e c c r r a

5 d l s c e a n

6 c e f e f t s

1 I bought a very unusual _____ costume _____ the other day. It was in the shape of a banana.

2 We laughed a lot at the play. It was a _____ .

3 The _____ liked the play very much and they clapped for a long time.

4 In Shakespeare's history plays, the main _____ are often kings and queens.

5 We didn't have any electricity last night. Mum lit _____ .

6 The special _____ in the play were amazing!

3 Complete the sentences with your own ideas.

1 I'll get _____ for you.

2 Sandra is angry. She's just heard that _____ .

3 I'll tell my best friend _____ .

4 My brother has just _____ .

What do I know?

1 **Read and tick ✓. Then write examples.**

1 I can make offers and promises with *will*. ☐

_____

_____

2 I can use the present perfect with *just*. ☐

_____

_____

3 I can write the names of five things that actors use. ☐

_____ _____ _____

_____ _____

2 🛡 **Write sentences to answer the Big Question.** **BIG QUESTION** **What do we know about the theatre?**

_____

_____

_____

My play

3 🛡 **Look at the pictures. Imagine your class has just performed *Romeo and Juliet*. Write about what happened.**

Think about: where you were.

what the actors were doing.

what suddenly happened.

what happened next.

_____

_____

_____

_____

_____

_____

1 Look and complete the words.

art ist

_____ eer

_____ woman

_____ er

_____ ic

_____ er

_____ ist

_____ er

2 Read and write the words from Activity 1.

1 Her paintings are wonderful.   _artist_

2 She repairs cars. _____

3 She looks after her animals. _____

4 He builds bridges. _____

5 She works for a big company and she travels a lot. _____

6 He cleans buildings before the people arrive. _____

7 He looks after your teeth. _____

8 He plans and draws how something will look. _____

1 Can you remember what the robot will do? Read and complete.

1 If I press the red button, it _____ the ground.

2 If I press the blue button, it _____ around.

3 If I press the green button, I don't know what it _____.

   Oh no! Achoo!

2 Read and match.

1 If you can't do your Maths homework, [f]   a I'll get an umbrella.

2 If the bus is late,   [ ]   b I'll wait for you.

3 If Music Club finishes late,   [ ]   c I'll dig a hole in the garden.

4 If you want to go out in the rain,   [ ]   d I'll take you to school in the car.

5 If you want to plant a tree,   [ ]   e I'll build you a rocket.

6 If you want to be an astronaut,   [ ]   f ~~I'll help you.~~

3 Read and complete. Use *will* and the verbs from the box.

repair   put up   carry   play   ~~fight~~   look it up

1 If you're scared of monsters, ___I'll fight___ them.

2 If you're bored, _____ with you.

3 If your bike is broken, _____ it for you.

4 If you don't know a word in English, _____ for you.

5 If you want to go camping, _____ the tent.

6 If your schoolbag is very heavy, _____ it for you.

4 Read the poem and then write your own.

If you're …

If you're sad,
I'll sing a song for you.
If you're angry,
I'll make you smile.
If you're scared,
I'll hold you in my arms.
And if you're happy,
I'll laugh with you.

If you're …

If you're sad,

_____.

If you're angry,

_____.

If you're scared,

_____.

And if you're happy,

_____.

1 Complete the sentences.

1 <u>I'd like to be</u> an artist.
2 _____ to do when you're older?
3 _____ cleaners in the future.
4 I'm not sure. _____ a designer.
5 _____ computer programmer.

I want to be a   There won't be any

~~I'd like to be~~   Maybe I'll be

What do you want

2 Put the dialogue in the correct order.

☐ **Robert** Really? There won't be any doctors in the future.

☐ **Robert** I'm not sure. Maybe I'll be a robot engineer.

☐ **Robert** I hope you're right.

[1] **Robert** What do you want to do when you're older?

☐ **Robert** Because we won't need them. Robots will do everything.

☐ **Emma** I think we'll need people for some things. Medicine is one of them.

☐ **Emma** So how about you? What do you want to be?

☐ **Emma** Why do you think that?

☐ **Emma** I'd like to be a doctor.

3 🎧 028 Listen and say the words.

they   think

They're thinking.

Phonics tip

The letters *th* can have the voiced sound: <u>they</u> or the unvoiced sound: <u>think</u>.

4 Read. Write the <u>underlined</u> words in the chart.

It was <u>Thelma</u>'s fa<u>th</u>er's bir<u>th</u>day on <u>Thursday</u>. Thelma wanted to buy him a lea<u>th</u>er belt, so her mo<u>th</u>er took her to a clo<u>th</u>es shop in town. While <u>they</u> were walking past <u>the</u> <u>th</u>eatre, she saw <u>that</u> *The Three Brothers* was playing <u>there</u>. Thelma <u>thought</u> going to see a play toge<u>th</u>er was the best <u>thing</u> she could give her father!

they	father,
think	Thelma,

5 🎧 029 Listen, check and say the words.

1 Put the lines of the chant in order. Write numbers (1–8).

Language focus

☐ Then I'll catch you.   ☐ But what if we fall in?

☐ That's all it takes.   ☐ Then we'll swim.

☐ But what if it breaks?   ☐ Let's cross the lake.

1 Let's cross the bridge.   ☐ That's not a problem.

2 Read and complete the dialogue with words from the box.

> food   visit   home   be   'll   what   ~~go~~

Dad Let's **(1)** __go__ to the museum.
Boy But **(2)** _____ if it is closed?
Dad Then we'll **(3)** _____ Grandpa.
Boy But what if he isn't at **(4)** _____?

Dad Then we **(5)** _____ go to a restaurant.
Boy But what if I don't like the **(6)** _____ there?
Dad Then you'll **(7)** _____ hungry for the rest of the day.

3 Write questions. Use a different verb for each question.

1 <u>What if the bridge breaks</u> ?
2 What _____ ?
3 _____ ?
4 _____ ?

4 Imagine you are the explorer in Activity 3. Choose two questions and write answers.

_____
_____
_____
_____

1 🛡 Remember the story. Who hides in or on these vehicles? Write names. There is one extra picture.

❶ 　　　　　 ❷ 　　　　　 ❸ 　　　　　 ❹

_____　_____　_____　_____

2 🛡 Read the summary and write the missing letters. Tick ✓ each letter in the grid below when you use it.

The children are in a muse _u_ m full of ama___ing cars and motorbik___s. They see a door with a sign that says, 'Don't e___ter', but Patrick de___ides to go in. The others ___ollow. Inside the room they hear a robo___ talking about ta___ing over the ___orld. They leave the room. ___uddenly they he___r someone callin___ for ___elp. They find a man trapped inside a su___marine. Patrick gets a bo___ of tools from the room with the models and they free the man.

His name is Don and his ___ob is to ___rogram the robots. He tells them that his best robot is ___angerous. He also tells the children about the on___y way to stop them. At exactl___ 6.55, while the ___obots are recharg___ng their batteries, Don and the children enter the co___puter room. D___n works ___uickly on a program to shut down the robots. It works and the world is sa___ed.

a	b	c	d	e	f	g	h	i	j	k	l	m
n	o	p	q	r	s	t	u ✓	v	w	x	y	z

3 Write questions for these answers.

1 What _do the children see in the museum_ _____?
They see sports cars and motorbikes.

2 What does _____?
It says, 'Don't enter'.

3 Where does _____?
He finds it in the room with the models in it.

4 What is _____?
His job is to program the robots.

5 What time _____?
They go there at exactly 6.55 a.m.

4   What message can we learn from the story in the Student's Book?
<u>Underline</u> the best summary.

a You shouldn't believe
a robot.

b You should try to
help people.

c Robots are never
helpful.

5 Match the exhibits of the future with the rooms in the museum. Then write four more items.

MUSIC	TRANSPORT	SCHOOL	FURNITURE	GADGETS
electric guitar				

6 Choose one of the items from Activity 5. Imagine what it will look like in the year 2531.
Draw a picture and write about it.

This is a bed from 2531. It has a computer
in it. If you can't get to sleep, it will play your
favourite music to help you. In the morning,
it wakes you up with breakfast. It then
puts your clothes on for you. They are nice
and warm. You never have to get out of bed
feeling cold or hungry!

1 🎧 030 **Listen and tick ☑. There is one example.**

1 What should Katy put on the table?

a
 ☐

b
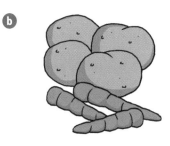 ☑

c
 ☐

2 Which is William's bike?

a
 ☐

b
 ☐

c
 ☐

3 What subjects will Richard's class study this morning?

a
 ☐

b
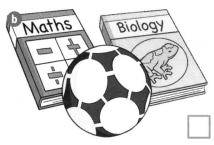 ☐

c
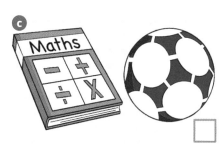 ☐

4 Where should Lucy put the notebook?

a
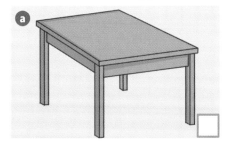 ☐

b
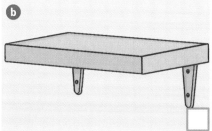 ☐

c
 ☐

5 Where has the teacher left his car keys?

a
 ☐

b
 ☐

c
 ☐

1 **Complete the story with five words from the box.**

great   car   nervous   opened   ~~games~~   closed   behind   rain   above   parents

My last birthday was really cool. Mum invited all my friends from my class. There were 12 boys and 8 girls. First, we played in the garden with my sister, Jane. Jane is 17. She knows lots of great **(1)** _____games_____. We had a fantastic time, but then it started to **(2)** _____. 'Why don't you come into the house?' my mum said. 'I'm sure you're all very hungry!' She was right. We were all very, very hungry. The food was **(3)** _____. We had hot dogs and drank orange juice, but there was more. We had the best birthday cake in the world! Yummy! Later, my sister said to me, 'Now you can look at your presents.' There was a big box with my name on it. I was so excited. When I **(4)** _____ it, I couldn't believe what I saw. In the box there was a robot. 'If you press the buttons,' my sister said, 'it'll do great things!' We went out into the garden again. 'Press the green button,' my friends said, but I didn't. I pressed the yellow button. The robot started to run very fast. It ran through the garden gate and down the street. 'Come back!' I shouted. But it didn't come back. The next morning, when I went to school, I saw the robot. It was lying **(5)** _____ a bush near the park. The battery was flat.

2 **Now choose the best name for the story. Tick ☑ one box.**

☐ That was great fun!   ☐ The birthday present   ☐ Playing with my sister

3 🛡 **Imagine you do one of these jobs. Then read and answer.**

fruit cleaner   pet detective   elephant dancer

ostrich babysitter   pet-food tester   golf-ball diver

1 How did you get interested in the job?

_____

_____

2 What do you like about the job?

_____

_____

3 How will the job be different in the future?

_____

_____

Think and learn

1 What can you remember about modern farming? Complete the sentences.

> Chemicals   crops   ~~machines~~   polytunnel   drone

1 In modern farming, lots of different ___machines___ are used to help the farmers.
2 The _____ need water to grow.
3 Sometimes, plants are grown inside a _____ .
4 _____ are used to stop insects eating the crops.
5 A _____ may be used to take photos from the sky.

2 Who are drones useful for? Look, think and tick ✓.

engineers and builders

emergency doctors

teachers

journalists

delivery companies

artists

3 Read. Were your predictions right?

DRONES – real-life robots!

Drones can do some amazing things. They are changing how people work and creating new job opportunities.
Drones are very good for taking photographs from the sky. More and more journalists and news programmes
are using them to take pictures of important events.

Photographs from the sky can also be very useful for engineers and builders when they are planning and
designing their projects.

Drones can be used to deliver letters and light packages. Most drones can't carry very heavy things,
like people, but they can reach places which are difficult or dangerous to travel to by road.

They can be useful in emergency situations. Drones have already been used to take photographs of disasters
so that medical workers know what they will see when they arrive. Now, they are taking medical equipment
and medicines to emergency situations too.

4 **Read the text about drones again. Write *t* (true), *f* (false) or *ds* (doesn't say).**

1 There is less work for people because of drones.   _f_

2 You could see pictures from a drone on TV.   ___

3 Drones can travel through water.   ___

4 Drones can travel to places that cars can't travel to.   ___

5 Drones can take doctors to emergency situations.   ___

6 Drones can help people connect to the Internet.   ___

5 **Look and write.**

1 How many more uses for drones can you think of?

_____

_____

2 What new jobs do you think drones have created?

_____

_____

6 **Project** **Think and write.**

Problems that farmers can have:

Ways a machine could help farmers:

1 **Choose six words or phrases to complete the sentences.**

Word box:
father says | don't do
~~will cook~~ | if Jane
do | will
will she do | comes
will be | say

1 If you are hungry, the robot _____will cook_____ a meal for you.
2 What will he do if his _____ no?
3 If Paul doesn't understand his homework, the robot _____ help him.
4 What _____ if her friend doesn't come?
5 What _____ doesn't like her present?
6 If I _____ my homework, the teacher will be angry.

2 **Join the pieces to make words and use them to complete the sentences.**

~~mech~~   farm   eng   chem   des   den

ineer   tist   igner   ~~anic~~   icals   er

1 I need a _____mechanic_____. My car has broken down.
2 One of my teeth hurts. I am seeing my _____ tomorrow.
3 Sue's mum is an _____. She builds aeroplanes.
4 Tom's dad is a _____. He has pigs, cows and chickens.
5 I'd love to be a _____. I have lots of ideas for making things.
6 Farmers sometimes use _____ on their crops.

3 **Complete the sentences with your own ideas.**

1 What will _____ doesn't give us any homework this weekend?
2 If it's sunny _____ the beach.
3 _____ we don't get any homework tonight?
4 What will she do _____?
5 I'll phone you later if _____.
6 If you're hungry _____.

What do I know?

1 **Read and tick ☑. Then write examples.**

1 I can write sentences with *if* clauses. ☐

_____

_____

2 I can write questions with *What if … ?* ☐

_____

_____

3 I can write the names of five jobs. ☐

_____ _____ _____

_____ _____

2 🛡 **Write sentences to answer the Big Question.** **BIG QUESTION** **How will jobs change in the future?**

_____

_____

_____

My journey

3 🛡 **Imagine that you and your friend went for a drive with your robot. Write what happened.**

Think about: where you went.

what you saw.

whether you enjoyed the ride.

what you all did when you got home.

_____

_____

_____

_____

_____

_____

_____

9 Mystery at sea

1 Do the crossword.

```
      1
²s  a  i  l  o  r              3

                 4     5
         6        7

   8

                 9
```

Across

2 He/She works on a ship.

4 The most important person on the ship.

6 It shows you what the weather will be like.

8 This is a small animal, but bigger than a mouse, with a long tail.

9 When the wind blows, the sailors put this up.

Down

1 You escape from a ship in this.

3 This is where you sleep on a ship.

5 This is a window in a ship.

7 This is a long pole where the sails are fastened.

2 Look at the picture. How many are there?

1 masts   three

2 sails   _____

3 portholes   _____

4 lifeboats   _____

5 sailors   _____

6 captains   _____

7 rats   _____

1 Read and circle the correct word.

1 I've **already** / yet seen a snake.   3 He's **already** / yet seen a bat.

2 But I haven't seen a hippo already / **yet**.   4 But he hasn't seen a zebra already / **yet**.

2 Read and complete. Use *already* and the present perfect form of the verbs from the box.

~~visit~~   have   be   see   do   listen

1 Daniel ___has already visited___ the new museum.

2 Holly and Cleo _____ their homework.

3 We _____ dinner – we're not hungry.

4 I _____ the film.

5 She _____ to Suzy Slick's new CD.

6 Mia _____ to Spain.

3 It's Dan's birthday. Write sentences about the things he has already done or hasn't done yet.

1 eat breakfast ✗ ___He hasn't eaten his breakfast yet.___

2 read all his birthday cards ✓ _____

3 open his birthday presents ✓ _____

4 tidy away all the paper ✗ _____

5 play his new game ✗ _____

6 talk to best friend on the phone ✓ _____

4 Read the poem. Write your own.

I've already visited sixty countries.

I've already learned ten languages.

I've already been to a hundred museums.

I've already been to the moon.

What next?

1 🛡 Remember the song. Complete the words to find out what Grandma was doing. Write the missing letters below.

1 f_uss   2 t_l_scope   3 Gran__ma   4 f__sh   5 fro__t

6 a__ain   7 cap__ain   8 anc__or   9 whal__

10 __oat   11 sa__l   12 __ubbed   13 __rop   14 __ea

F __ __ __ __ __ __ __ __   __ __ __ __   __ __ __ __ __ __

2 🎧 031 Listen and order. Write the numbers.

☐ Some sailors jumped into the water to look for Grandma.

☐ Suddenly Grandma was standing next to Jimmy and asked, 'What's all the fuss about?'

☐ The captain dropped the anchor.

☐ Jimmy ran to the telescope to check where Grandma was.

1 Grandma was standing beside Jimmy on the ship. Both were looking out at the sea.

☐ When Jimmy turned around Grandma was not there any more.

☐ Jimmy thought his grandma might be inside a whale.

3 🎧 032 Listen and say the words.

foot   could   boot   you

Phonics tip

The short sound in f**oo**t is the same as in p**u**t and c**ou**ld. The long sound in b**oo**t is the same as in z**oo** or y**ou**.

4 Write the words in the correct column.

~~put~~ ~~moon~~ should woman rule pull soup choose wood glue pool school would stood blew took

foot	boot
put	moon

5 🎧 033 Listen, check and say the words.

1 Put a mark (^) where *yet* should go in each line.

Language focus

Have you put on your boots^?

My boots? No, I haven't. I haven't done that.

Have you packed your bag?

My bag? No, I haven't. I haven't done that.

2 Make questions.

1 dog / Have / walked / yet / you / the / ?
  <u>Have you walked the dog yet?</u>

2 tried / you / bike / Have / out / new / yet / Mia's / ?
  _____

3 seen / you / new / *Treasure Island* / the / Have / film / yet / ?
  _____

4 you / yet / your / tidied / Have / room / ?
  _____

3 Read and write answers.

1 Have you read the last Harry Potter book yet? (No / see the film)
  <u>No, I haven't read the last Harry Potter book yet, but I've already seen the film.</u>

2 Have you been to New York yet? (No / go to Los Angeles)
  _____

3 Have you fed the cat yet? (No / tidy bedroom)
  _____

4 Have the Bensons sold their house yet? (No / sell car)
  _____

4 Look and write.

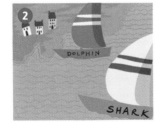

1 Tom <u>has already had a bath, but Harry hasn't had a bath yet.</u>

2 The *Dolphin* _____

3 He _____

4 She _____

1 Remember the story. Look at the pictures and complete the summary.

The children are on a big sailing ship. The sailors don't look very friendly, so <u>they</u> hide in a

(1) __lifeboat__ . Unfortunately, Patrick sneezes and some (2) _____ find them. They take the children

5 to the (3) _____, who tells the sailors to lock them in his (4) _____. <u>He</u> seems very worried.

Inside the cabin, Phoebe finds the captain's

(5) _____. <u>It</u> says that he thinks something strange is going to happen. Patrick tells <u>them</u> to come and

10 look out of the (6) _____. Outside, they can see a light, but it's not yellow like their gate, it's green. The children decide to escape and break down the door with a (7) _____. They race outside. There are lots of green lights on the ship and the sailors

15 are walking through <u>them</u> and disappearing. Alex then remembers about the *Mary Celeste*, a ship that was found with no-one on <u>it</u>. Then they see the yellow glow of their gate. They walk through <u>it</u> and find that <u>they</u> are back in the (8) _____ of their school.

20 Home at last … or … are they?

2 Read the summary in Activity 1 again. Who or what do the <u>underlined</u> words refer to?

1 they (line 2) ____the children____
2 He (line 6) _____
3 It (line 8) _____
4 them (line 9) _____
5 them (line 15) _____
6 it (line 17) _____
7 it (line 18) _____
8 they (line 19) _____

3 Read and write answers.

1 Where are the children?

   They are on a big sailing boat.

2 Why does the sailor find the children?

   _____
   _____

3 What do the children read?

   _____
   _____

4 Why does Patrick tell the other two to come to the porthole?

   _____
   _____

5 Why are the children careful not to walk into a green light?

   _____
   _____

6 Why do the children think that something is wrong when they get back to school?

   _____
   _____

4 **Read the captain's diary and write the missing words. Write one word on each line.**

Things are strange. There is something wrong with this ship. I have a strong feeling that something bad is going to happen to my ship and my men.

Last night, I had a dream. It was a very strange dream, a terrible dream. There were **(1)** ____green____ lights all over the ship.

My men and I walked into them. We didn't want to, but we **(2)** _____ stop – we had to walk.

We walked through the lights and suddenly we were in a very strange place. We weren't on the **(3)** _____ any more. We were on dry land. We **(4)** _____ on the side of a mountain and there was

(5) _____ coming from the top of it. I looked **(6)** _____ my men. They were frightened. Below us, we could see a small town. It wasn't like any town I have ever seen. Suddenly, there was a huge **(7)** _____ and a giant fireball shot out of the mountain into the sky.

And that is when I woke up. I know it was only a dream, but it seemed so real. This **(8)** _____ when I woke up, I found the ship's cat was missing. She is my lucky charm and now I am afraid for the safety of my **(9)** _____ and my men.

5 **Imagine you are the captain. Write a message to send for help.**

6 **Which places and times would you like to visit if you were on a boat? Write a list.**

I want to go to Roman times in 750BCE.

1 Look and read. Write 1–4 words to complete the sentences about the story.

Grace Darling was born in 1815. She had five brothers and three sisters. When she was ten, her family moved to the island of Longstone on the northern coast of England. On the island, there was a lighthouse and Grace's father was the lighthouse keeper. All the children helped their father to check the lamps.

Some years later, her brothers and sisters left the island to get jobs. Only one brother stayed on the island with Grace and her parents.

On the night of Wednesday 5th September, a ship left the city of Hull. There were 60 people on board. On Thursday, the engines stopped in a storm and the captain could not start them again. Early on Friday morning, the ship hit the rocks of a small island. The ship broke and 40 people fell into the icy water. The ship had a lifeboat, but only a few people could get into it.

On Thursday night, the Darling family could hear the storm and when they looked out of their home in the morning, they could see the broken ship. They could also see nine people who were holding on to the rocks. Grace's brother was away, so Grace knew that only she and her father could save the people on the rocks.

Grace and her father got into their wooden boat and after a long time, they reached the people on the rock. As they got near to the rock, her father jumped out to help the people. Grace stayed in the boat. She rowed very hard so that the waves didn't throw the boat against the rocks. They put five people into the boat and rowed to the lighthouse. Then they made the trip again to save the rest of the people.

Grace and her father became very famous. The town gave Grace a gold medal, the story was in all the papers, and she had lots of presents from people.

1 Grace's _____parents_____ had nine children.

2 Grace's family moved to an island when Grace _____.

3 When Grace was older, only _____ stayed with Grace and their parents on the island.

4 The ship left Hull with _____ on board.

5 When the ship hit the rocks, it _____.

6 Only a few people managed to _____.

7 Grace and her father _____ nine people.

8 People read about Grace in the newspaper and sent her _____.

2 What values do you think Grace Darling showed? Read and circle.

being brave   being honest   not giving up   helping people   respecting other cultures

1 🎧 034 **Listen to the radio show again. Read and match.**

1 Sirens were women who — c

2 The Kraken is a huge octopus

3 Scientists have found

4 The Loch Ness Monster doesn't

5 Many people have tried

a that sinks ships.

b a giant octopus.

c ~~sat on rocks and sang beautifully.~~

d live in the sea.

e to take photos of the Loch Ness Monster.

2 **Write about the 'Jammlup' and say what it does.**

_____

3 **Look, read and think. Is the diver telling the truth? Why? / Why not?**

A diver said he found a very old vase in the sea. On the vase were the numbers and letters 312BCE.

_____

Think and learn

1 🛡 **Look and complete the chart.** ~~breathe~~ fish lay mammals reptiles warm

	(4) _____	(5) _____	(6) _____
(1) ___breathe___ underwater	✗	✗	✓
(2) _____ -blooded	✓	✗	✗
(3) _____ eggs	✗	✓	✓
give milk to their babies	✓	✗	✗
have scales	✗	✓	✓
examples:	_____ _____	_____ _____	_____ _____

2 What animals can you remember? Add some examples to the chart in Activity 1.

3 Why do animals use camouflage? Look, read and tick ☑ the reasons mentioned in the text.

KINGS OF CAMOUFLAGE!

Many fish have amazing camouflage. Let's take a look at some.

What can you see – a plant or a fish? It looks like a plant and moves like a plant, but the leafy seadragon is actually a fish! It can't swim very well, so it uses camouflage to hide from animals that want to eat it.

You can hardly see the leaf scorpionfish against the coral reef where it lives, but it is one of the most dangerous fish in the sea. It acts like a leaf so that it can hide from animals it wants to eat.

The cuttlefish can change shape and colour to hide from danger. It can make itself look like a piece of coral, a plant, or even the sand at the bottom of the sea!

to hide from danger ☐   to look for food without being seen ☐   to find friends ☐
to show other animals it is there ☐   to look pretty ☐

4 Read about more marine animals and answer *t* (true) or *f* (false).

GIANTS OF THE OCEAN!

There are certainly some dangerous and unusual animals in the ocean, but did you know that some of the world's biggest animals also live there?

The whale shark is the biggest fish of all. Although it can be 12 metres long, it mostly eats small fish and other tiny sea creatures. It catches them by swimming along with its mouth open!

The largest reptile on Earth is the saltwater crocodile, which also lives in the sea. It can be up to 6 metres long. It eats anything it can find – including monkeys and even sharks. Some people say it is the animal most likely to eat a human!

The ocean is also home to the largest creature ever to live: the blue whale. A baby blue whale can be over 7 metres long, but adults can grow to 30 metres long. They can weigh more than 130,000 kg. That's longer than three buses and heavier than three lorries! The blue whale also eats tiny sea creatures – around 40 million of them every day!

1 The whale shark eats other sharks.   f
2 A baby blue whale is longer than a saltwater crocodile.   _____
3 The blue whale is the biggest animal of all.   _____
4 The saltwater crocodile is longer than the whale shark.   _____
5 The whale shark is a fish.   _____
6 The saltwater crocodile is not a meat-eater.   _____

5 Choose one of the animals in Activity 4 and complete the fact file.

Marine animal: _____
Type of animal: _____
Size: _____
Eats: _____
Unusual fact: _____

6   **Project Read and answer.**

1 What animal did you choose?
_____

2 Is it a reptile, a fish or a mammal?
_____

3 Write three facts you found out about it:
_____
_____
_____
_____

1 Draw lines and complete the sentences with words from the box.

> tidied up   We   hasn't been   new film   haven't   ~~done~~

1 My sister has   the _____   bedroom yet?

2 Have they seen   been to the USA, but   yet.

3 I _____   _____ your   her homework.

4 Have you   already ___done___   he _____ to New York yet.

5 He's   done our homework   yet?

6 _____ haven't eaten my   soup yet.

2 Find the words and use them to complete the sentences.

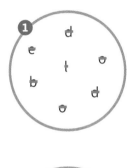

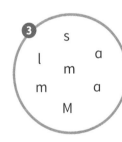

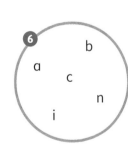

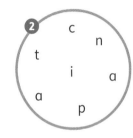

1 Warm-_____blooded_____ animals can stay hot when it is cold.

2 When we got on board, the _____ showed us his ship.

3 _____ feed their babies milk.

4 A _____ is used to rescue people.

5 When we looked through the _____, we could see the big waves.

6 Sailors sleep in a _____ on ships.

3 Complete the sentences with your own ideas.

1 This week, I've already _____.

2 This week, I haven't _____ yet.

3 This month, my friend has already _____.

4 My friend hasn't _____ yet.

5 This year, my family and I have already _____.

6 We haven't _____ yet.

1 **Read and tick ✓. Then write examples.**

1 I can write sentences with *already* and *yet*. ☐
_____
_____

2 I can write questions with *Have you … yet?* ☐
_____
_____

3 I can write the names of five things on board a boat or ship. ☐
_____ _____ _____
_____ _____

2 Write sentences to answer the Big Question.

BIG QUESTION **What do we know about the sea?**
_____
_____
_____

3 **Look at the pictures. Imagine you are one of the people on the sailing ship. Write the story.**

Think about: where you were.
what the weather was like.
how people were feeling.
what happened.

_____
_____
_____
_____
_____
_____
_____
_____

1 Filling in a form

- When you fill in a form, follow all the instructions carefully.
- Sometimes you have to write in small spaces, so your writing should be tidy.

1 Complete the instructions on Eva's form with the phrases from the box.

> 20–30 words   ~~black~~   CAPITAL LETTERS
> Circle   Underline   YYYY

HARDWICK HOUSE Language School

Please complete this form with a **(1)** __black__ *pen.*

ABOUT YOU
Please complete this section in **(2)** _____.

Last name: | SANTOS
First name: | EVA

Date of birth: D D   M M   **(3)** _____
28 | 03 | 2002

DATES FOR YOUR LANGUAGE COURSE
(4) _____ the right month.

(December)   January   July   August

OTHER SUMMER SCHOOL ACTIVITIES
(5) _____ three activities:

swimming   tennis   painting   football
volleyball   singing   cooking   hiking

YOUR LANGUAGES
Tell us about the languages you speak.

Write **(6)** _____.

I speak Spanish at home with my family and I started English lessons when I was six. I know some French words because my grandmother is French.

2 Read the instructions carefully and complete the form with your information.

Tottlebank Language School

Please complete this form in BLUE.

YOUR DETAILS
Please use CAPITAL LETTERS.

First name: _____

Last name: _____

Date of birth: DD   MM   YYYY
[ ]   [ ]   [   ]

CIRCLE THE MONTH OF THE COURSE
January   July   August   December

OTHER ACTIVITIES ON YOUR COURSE
Underline your two favourite activities:
volleyball   singing   cooking   hiking
swimming   tennis   painting   football

YOU AND LANGUAGES
Write 15–25 words about the languages you speak.

_____
_____
_____
_____

Check your writing

- Did you use the correct colour? _____
- Did you circle and underline correctly? _____
- How many words are there in your last answer? _____ words

2 A description

Tips for writers

- When you write a description, use *who*, *which* and *where* to give more information.
- Use different adjectives to make your work more interesting.

1 Complete Ryan's description with the phrases from the box.

> who calls the restaurant   who is sitting
> which Auntie Sue always makes
> ~~where you can have parties~~
> which is from all the family   which plays music

B *I* U ☰ ☰ ☰ ☰

When it's Grandma's birthday, we all go to a nice restaurant with a special room **(1)** where you can have parties. Uncle Andrew is usually the one **(2)** _____ and he tells them how many people are going to come. It's always a nice meal and we finish with a nice cake, **(3)** _____ . Every year, we sit in different places, but the person **(4)** _____ next to Grandma gives her a nice present, **(5)** _____ . Last year, it was my turn. We gave Grandma a very old machine from the 1920s **(6)** _____ and we all danced! It was an unusual and noisy present, but she loved it.

📎

2 Ryan uses the adjective *nice* four times. Find and rewrite the phrases with different adjectives. Use a dictionary to help you. Remember to change *a* to *an* before a vowel sound.

1   a nice restaurant 〉 an amazing restaurant
2   _____
3   _____
4   _____

3 Describe or imagine something which you enjoy as a family: a special meal, a festival, a holiday, or your own ideas. Use *who*, *which*, *where* and different adjectives to make your work interesting.

B *I* U ☰ ☰ ☰ ☰

_____
_____
_____
_____
_____
_____
_____
_____
_____
_____
_____
_____
_____
_____
_____
_____
_____
_____
_____
_____

📎

Check your writing

- How many times did you use *who*, *which* or *where*? _____
- How many different adjectives did you use? _____

3 Plans for a trip

- When you talk about the future with *before*, *after* and *when*, use verbs in the present.

1 Complete the notice about the school trip with the verbs in brackets. Use *going to*, but remember to use the present simple with *before*, *after* and *when*.

Year 5 Day Trip to Cogges Farm

Weds 22nd May

Classes 5A and 5B (1) __are going to visit__ (visit) Cogges Farm next Wednesday.

Before you (2) _____ (get) on the bus, you must show Mr York your boots in a plastic bag. There's lots of mud at the farm!

When we (3) _____ (arrive), we (4) _____ (join) the School Time Travellers' programme. First, we (5) _____ (learn) how they built the farm in the 13th century and how people cooked their food here in the 19th century.

Then it's time for lunch in the café.

After we (6) _____ (finish) lunch, the head farmer (7) _____ (take) us on a tour of the farm. We (8) _____ (meet) some new piglets and lots of other animals. Finally, we (9) _____ (plant) some vegetables to learn about what plants need. Before we (10) _____ (come) back to school, you can visit the shop to buy souvenirs.

2 Imagine that you're going on a school trip. Write a notice for the school board. Use *going to* and *before*, *after* and *when* with the correct verb forms.

- Did you use these time expressions?
  ☐ *before* ☐ *after* ☐ *when*
- What tenses did you use?
  _____

4 An experiment

1 Read the report of an experiment in a Science lesson. Match the verbs with the definitions.

B *I* U ☰ ☰ ☰ ☰

Our seeds experiment

We collected a cardboard box, a plastic box and two plastic bottles and our teacher gave us four seeds. We put one seed in the cardboard box, where it didn't have any light or water. We put one seed in the plastic box and added two tablespoons of water. We put another seed in a plastic bottle, but we didn't add water. Then we put the last seed in a plastic bottle with two tablespoons of water. We monitored the size of the seeds every day for a week and we recorded the results in our notebooks. We found that the seed which had light and water was the biggest at the end of the week.

We concluded from this that seeds need light and water to grow. Next week, we're going to experiment with seeds in a hot place and a cold place to observe the effect of temperature.

🖉

1 monitor ☐   a test something

2 record ☐   b see or watch

3 conclude ☐   c decide that something is true

4 experiment ☐   d make notes

5 observe ☐   e check more than once (to look for changes)

2 Imagine that you did an experiment. Write a report. Use the words from Activity 1.

B *I* U ☰ ☰ ☰ ☰

_____
_____
_____
_____
_____
_____
_____
_____
_____
_____
_____
_____
_____
_____
_____
_____
_____

🖉

Check your writing

- How many words from Activity 1 did you use? _____
- Are your past tense verbs correct? _____
- Swap reports with a partner. Does your partner understand how to do your experiment? _____

5 Write a story

- Use the exact words that people say to make a story interesting. We call this 'direct speech'.
- Use different verbs of speech to show **how** people say things (for example, *shout* or *laugh*) or what their words mean (for example, *promise* or *offer*).
- Use speech marks and commas, but don't add commas if the direct speech ends with a question mark or an exclamation mark. *'Help!' he shouted.*

1 **Put the story in order.**

a ☐ Great idea! I'll be Rooney,' said Dylan.

b ☐ Dylan kicked the ball very high and it flew towards their neighbour's house. Crash! 'Oh no! Mr Curry's window!' said Adam.

c ☐ 'It's too late to mend a window on a Sunday evening, but I've got some flat wood in the garage. I'll cover the window for you and it will be safe until tomorrow,' their dad offered.

d ☐1 'Let's play football!' suggested Adam.

e ☐ Dylan's dad was washing the car when he heard the crash and Mr Curry's voice, so he went to speak to his neighbour.

f ☐ 'Shhh! Mr Curry's coming out,' whispered Dylan. 'Quick! Let's hide in the garage. Maybe he won't know that it was us.'

g ☐ 'You? Rooney? OK, and I'll be Messi!' laughed Adam and the two boys started playing.

h ☐ While they were going into the garage, Mr Curry came out of his house. He had their ball in his hands and he looked at the glass on the ground. 'Dylan! Adam! Was that you?' he shouted angrily.

i ☐ 'Oh, Adam and Dylan will pay for the window,' their dad promised. 'Did you hear that, boys? Come out of the garage NOW and bring that flat wood with you. You're going to help me.'

j ☐ 'Thank you,' said Mr Curry, 'but what about tomorrow? Who's going to pay for the window?'

2 **Complete the verbs of speech from the story.**

1 l a u g h ed   4 o _ _ _ _ _ ed
2 p _ _ _ _ _ ed   5 s _ _ _ _ _ _ ed
3 w _ _ _ _ _ _ _ ed   6 s _ _ _ _ ed

3 Write a story about Billie Liar from Student's Book page 60. You can invent details. Use direct speech in your story. Remember to use speech marks and different verbs of speech. Add commas where necessary.

_____
_____
_____
_____
_____
_____
_____
_____
_____
_____
_____
_____
_____
_____
_____
_____
_____

- How many different verbs of speech did you use? _____
- Did you use commas and speech marks where necessary? _____

6 Helping a friend

- When a friend asks you for advice, give ideas with *should* and other language to sound friendly.

  ~~Talk to more people.~~
  You should talk to more people.
  Try to talk to more people.
  Why don't you talk to more people?
  Maybe you should talk to more people?

1 Luke is a new boy at Kirkston School. He explained on a school web forum that he wasn't happy. Read his classmates' emails and complete the sentences below.

●●●

A I'm sorry that you're sad. I moved from a new town and I wasn't happy at first. You should talk to more people. You'll make new friends soon.

B Try not to worry. It's always difficult to start a new school. Maybe you shouldn't read every breaktime? You should try to talk to more people. Then you can find friends who like the same things as you. Why not join an after-school club? I'm sure you'll make new friends soon.

C Why don't you like our school? Make more friends. Talk to people at breaktime. Don't worry. You're sad because you don't try. That's silly.

1 Email ☐ doesn't help at all.

2 Email ☐ is kind, but it doesn't help much.

3 Email ☐ is the best because it gives good ideas.

2 Complete these friendly ways of giving advice from the best email in Activity 1.

1 _____ _____ _____ worry.

2 _____ _____ _____ read every breaktime?

3 _____ _____ _____ an after-school club?

3 Make this advice friendly.

1 It's wrong to be sad.

  Try not to be sad.

2 Join the school team.

  _____

3 Talk to a teacher.

  _____

4 You'll be OK.

  _____

4 Read the situation. Write an email giving advice in a friendly way.

A new boy/girl is scared of someone in your class who always says horrible things. This person sits with the new boy/girl at lunchtime and asks for sweets. The new boy/girl can't say no. Now the person is asking for money. The new boy/girl asks you for advice.

_____

_____

_____

_____

_____

_____

_____

- How many different ways did you use to sound friendly? _____
- Swap emails with a partner. Does your partner think your advice is good? _____

7 A biography

1 Look at the notes about Cervantes, a famous Spanish writer. Complete the biography.

Miguel de Cervantes

1547: Born Alcalá de Henares, near Madrid. Six brothers and sisters; his father was a travelling doctor

1567: Studied for a year at a college in Madrid

1569: Went to work for a rich man in Italy

1570: Joined the Spanish army

1571: Hurt his left hand and couldn't use it again

1575–80: In prison for 5 years, got ideas for his books

1584: Got married

1588: Got a job in the south of Spain

1605: Wrote Part 1 of *Don Quijote*

1609–16: Lived in Madrid, wrote short novels

1614: Another author wrote Part 2 for *Don Quijote*

1615: Cervantes wrote his Part 2

1616: Died (The same day as Shakespeare? No-one knows.)

Cervantes **(1)** was born in 1547. At the age of **(2)** _____ in Madrid. After that, he **(3)** _____. In 1570, he **(4)** _____, but a year later, he **(5)** _____. He spent five years **(6)** _____ from 1575 to 1580, which gave him **(7)** _____. Cervantes **(8)** _____ in 1584 and four years later, **(9)** _____.

(10) _____ Part 1 of his most famous book, *Don Quijote*, and then from 1609 to 1616, **(11)** _____, where he wrote short novels. In 1614, another author **(12)** _____, so Cervantes **(13)** _____ a year later. He died **(14)** _____, possibly on the same day as Shakespeare, but **(15)** _____.

2 Interview an older relative or ask your mum or dad about someone. Write a biography. Use time phrases to vary your sentences.

8 An advertisement

Do you hate writing? Do you need a faster way to write?

If you want to do your homework more quickly, you'll love the Think-write-o-matic! You wear it like an MP3 player with earphones, but it's smaller than a mobile phone.

This amazing gadget 'reads' the ideas in your head and writes on a computer as quickly as you think!

The best homework invention of the 21st century!

1 Read the advertisement. Are the sentences below *t* (true) or *f* (false)?

1 This gadget is for people who write slowly.   _t_
2 It's bigger than a mobile phone.   ____
3 It writes more quickly than you can think.   ____

2 Write *If* clauses to complete these advertisements. Use your own ideas with the words from the box.

> ~~don't like …~~   want to …   more quickly
> need a better way to …   hate (+ -ing)

If you   __don't like walking your dog, you'll want__
the Dog-walk-o-matic! [€89.99]

_____,
you'll love the Bedroom-tidy-o-matic! [€149.99]

_____,
you'll need the Cook-o-matic! [€299.99]

3 Complete the sentences with the names of the gadgets from Activity 2 and comparative or superlative forms.

1 The _Cook-o-matic_ is the most expensive gadget.
2 The Bedroom-tidy-o-matic is _____ than the Cook-o-matic.
3 The _____ is the best way to exercise your pet.
4 The _____ invention is the Dog-walk-o-matic.

4 Invent an amazing gadget. Write an advertisement using a first conditional and comparative and superlative forms.

Check your writing

- Did you explain who will want your product? ____
- How many forms did you use? comparative ____ superlative ____
- Compare your advertisements in groups. Which other gadgets do you like? ____

9 A summary

1 Read the story on Student's Book pages 86–87 again. Tick ✓ the eight most important things that happen in the story.

a ☐ Phoebe says, 'Let's go and talk to Shakespeare'.

b ☐ The friends climb onto the stage.

c ☐ Shakespeare was sitting on a big box.

d ✓ Phoebe tells Shakespeare that they can help.

e ☐ Two angry men arrive, but the three friends save Shakespeare from them.

f ☐ The two men shout, 'Give us our money back!'

g ☐ With a loud crash, the two men fell off the stage.

h ☐ He invites the children home for dinner.

i ☐ Phoebe suggests a different ending.

j ☐ They hear voices and Shakespeare opens the door.

k ☐ The two men from the theatre arrive with some of their friends.

l ☐ One man knows that Patrick had the sword.

m ☐ The men are angry, but Shakespeare invites them to come and see the new ending.

n ☐ At the end of the play, the audience claps and Shakespeare is happy.

o ☐ The children see the gate on the stage and step through it.

2 Look at Student's Book page 82. Which of these opening sentences tells you the most important things at the start of this episode?

1 ☐ Phoebe is talking about studying Shakespeare in English lessons.

2 ☐ The Time Travellers are watching the end of *Romeo and Juliet* in The Globe Theatre, but the audience don't like it.

3 ☐ The three friends are in The Globe Theatre and the actor in tights is holding hands with the actress.

3 Choose the story on Student's Book pages 98–99 or pages 110–111. Make notes about the important things that happen.

_____

_____

_____

_____

4 Now write an opening sentence for the story that you chose in Activity 3. Use 15–25 words.

_____

_____

_____

_____

Check your writing

- How many words did you use? _____
- Did you talk about who, where and what? _____
- Find a partner who chose the same story. Did you use the same details?

  Yes _____   No _____

  I wrote about _____ and my partner wrote about _____.

Verb	Past	Past participle
be	was/were	been
become	became	become
begin	began	begun
bet	bet	bet
break	broke	broken
bring	brought	brought
build	built	built
buy	bought	bought
choose	chose	chosen
come	came	come
come out	came out	come out
cry	cried	cried
cut	cut	cut
cut down	cut down	cut down
cut out	cut out	cut out
die	died	died
dig	dug	dug
do	did	done
draw	drew	drawn
drink	drank	drunk
drive	drove	driven
drive away	drove away	driven away
eat	ate	eaten
fall	fell	fallen
fall off	fell off	fallen off
feed	fed	fed
feel	felt	felt
find	found	found
find out	found out	found out
fly	flew	flown
forget	forgot	forgotten
get	got	got
get out	got out	got out
get up	got up	got up
give	gave	given
go	went	gone
grow	grew	grown
grow up	grew up	grown up
have	had	had
hear	heard	heard
hide	hid	hidden
hold	held	held
keep	kept	kept
know	knew	known

Verb	Past	Past participle
lay	laid	laid
leave	left	left
lie	lay	lain
lose	lost	lost
make	made	made
mean	meant	meant
meet	met	met
pay	paid	paid
put	put	put
read	read	read
resell	resold	resold
ride	rode	ridden
run	ran	run
run away	ran away	run away
run down	ran down	run down
say	said	said
see	saw	seen
sell	sold	sold
serve	served	served
shut down	shut down	shut down
sing	sang	sung
sit	sat	sat
sit down	sat down	sat down
sleep	slept	slept
spend	spent	spent
spit out	spat out	spat out
stand	stood	stood
steal	stole	stolen
stick	stuck	stuck
sweep	swept	swept
swing	swung	swung
take	took	taken
take off	took off	taken off
tear	tore	torn
tell	told	told
think	thought	thought
throw	threw	thrown
tidy	tidied	tidied
tie	tied	tied
try	tried	tried
wake up	woke up	woken up
wear	wore	worn
win	won	won
write	wrote	written